Arizona Rivers and Streams Guide

Arizona Rivers and Streams Guide

First Printing 1989
Second Printing 1993
Third Printing 1995
Fourth Printing 1998

This guide was produced for Arizona State Parks, with money from the State Lake Improvement Fund, by Recreative Ink, a Flagstaff based publishing firm. Recreative Ink specializes in preparing guides, informative literature, and computer programs on outdoor (recreative) activities.

The bulk of the research for this guide, and all the writing was done by Dan Dagget. The maps were drawn by Dawson Henderson, with help from Ed Locke. The layout, editing and typesetting were by Ken Walters of Gneiss Structures.

Cover Design by Paul Mirocha and Tanna Thornburg

Cover photo of the Salt River by Kenneth Walters

Section photos:

Introduction	Salome Creek	Dan Dagget	
Northern	Colorado River	Kenneth Walters	pg 18
Western	Bill Williams River	Tanna Thornburg	pg 44
	Colorado River	Tanna Thornburg	pg 44
Southern	Aravaipa Creek	Tanna Thornburg	pg 62
Eastern	White River—East Fork	Dan Dagget	pg 86
Central	Verde River	Charles Eatherly	pg 130
	West Clear Creek	Tanna Thornburg	pg 130
Appendix	Black River	Tanna Thornburg	pg 176

Camera-ready copy was produced with Apple® Macintosh™ computers and Apple® LaserWriter IINT™ printers, using Microsoft Word, Adobe Illustrator 88, and Aldus PageMaker. The font used is Palatino.

Arizona State Parks
1300 West Washington
Phoenix, AZ 85007

(602) 542-4174
(800) 285-3703
from 520 area code

http://www.pr.state.az.us

This document is available in alternative
formats by contacting the Public
Information Officer.

CONTENTS

Introduction
 We'll Lead You To Water 1
 Whitewater Boating Classification 13
 Icon Key 14
 Map Symbols 15
 Streams at a Glance 16
Northern Rivers and Streams 19
 Canyon de Chelly 20
 Chevelon Creek 22
 Colorado River - Glen Canyon...24
 Colorado River - Grand Canyon..26
 Colorado River - Western Grand Canyon 28
 East Clear Creek 30
 Havasu Creek 32
 Little Colorado - Headwaters to Forest Boundary 34
 Little Colorado - Grand Falls to Cameron 36
 Little Colorado - Cameron to Grand Canyon 38
 Paria River 40
 Virgin River - Virgin River Gorge 42
Western Rivers and Streams 45
 Bill Williams River 46
 Burro Creek - Florence Creek to US 93 48
 Colorado River - Black Canyon 50
 Colorado River - Davis Dam to Lake Havasu 52
 Colorado River - Parker Dam to Ehrenberg............................54
 Colorado River - Ehrenberg to Imperial Dam 56
 Colorado River - Laguna Dam to Morelos Dam 58
 Santa Maria River..60
Southern Rivers and Streams 63
 Aravaipa Creek 64
 Cave Creek - Chiricahuas 66
 Cienega Creek..68
 Gardner Canyon 70
 Hot Springs Canyon 72
 Madera Canyon 74
 Redfield Canyon 76
 Sabino Creek 78
 San Pedro River - International Boundary to Benson............80
 Sonoita Creek...82
 Sycamore Creek - Pajaritos 84
Eastern Rivers and Streams 87
 Big Bonito Creek 88
 Black River - East Fork 90

Black River - West Fork to Reservation Boundary 92
Black River - Reservation Boundary to White Confluence 94
Blue River - Blue Crossing to FR 475 96
Bonita Creek - Reservation Boundary to Gila Confluence 98
Canyon Creek 100
Cherry Creek 102
Cibeque Creek 104
Eagle Creek 106
Gila River - US 666 Bridge to Bonita Creek 108
Gila River - Coolidge Dam to Winkelman 110
Gila River - Kelvin to Ashurst-Hayden Dam 112
Salt River - US 60 to Gleason Flats 114
Salt River - Gleason Flats to Horseshoe Bend 116
Salt River - Horseshoe Bend to Diversion Dam 118
Salt River - Stewart Mtn Dam to Granite Reef Dam 120
San Francisco River - Hot Springs to Clifton 122
San Francisco River - Clifton to Gila River 124
White River - North Fork 126
White River - East Fork 128
Central Rivers and Streams 131
Agua Fria River 132
Cave Creek 134
East Verde River 136
Fossil Creek 138
Granite Creek 140
Hassayampa River 142
Oak Creek - Pumphouse Wash to Sedona 144
Oak Creek - Sedona to Verde River 146
Salome Creek 148
Sycamore Creek 150
Tonto Creek - Fish Hatchery to Gisela 152
Tonto Creek - Gisela to Rye Creek 154
Tonto Creek - Rye Creek to Roosevelt 156
Verde River - Perkinsville to Clarkdale 158
Verde River - Clarkdale to Camp Verde 160
Verde River - Camp Verde to Beasley Flats 162
Verde River - Beasley Flats to Childs 164
Verde River - Childs to Horseshoe Reservoir 166
Verde River - Horseshoe Dam to Bartlett Reservoir 168
Verde River - Bartlett Dam to Salt River 170
West Clear Creek 172
Wet Beaver Creek 174

APPENDIX: Information Sources 177
INDEX 180

ACKNOWLEDGEMENTS

Because there are too many of you to thank in person, we'd like to take this opportunity to express our sincere appreciation to all the people who helped make this book possible. Thanks for answering our questions even when they didn't seem to make sense; for returning our calls when we didn't remember why we called you in the first place; and for supplying all those fantastic descriptions of indescribable places. Even under those circumstances many of you managed to respond with a touch of humor. We were happy for the opportunity to laugh along with you.

Help in putting together the information for this book came from a number of sources, including most of the national forest ranger districts in the state and several of the Bureau of Land Management district offices. State and local agencies such as the Arizona Game and Fish Department, the Pinal County Sheriff's Office in Florence, and the Parks and Recreation Departments of Pima County and the City of Prescott played a vital role. The White Mountain and San Carlos Apaches and the Navajo Tribe provided valuable information on the rivers that flow through their beautiful tribal lands. The Nature Conservancy was an indispensable source not only on the streams within their preserves but on areas along other streams as well.

To that already long list, a few individuals should be singled out for special acknowledgement. John Parsons, and George Marsik provided vital, in-depth information and even made it possible for us to get some first hand experience of the new sport of low water boating. Doyen Salsig did a great job of proof reading, making sure you don't have to navigate through treacherous shoals of typos while gaining access to the information that others helped us gather.

Last but not least, some credit must be paid to the magnificent riparian areas that bless the state of Arizona and that are the subject of this book. Even though only ten percent of the riparian areas we once had still remain, they nevertheless stand as one of Arizona's greatest treasures. Getting to know this rare and irreplaceable resource, made doing the research for this guide as much fun as you will have using it.

Publications Order Form

ITEM	DESCRIPTION	PRICE	QUANTITY	TOTAL
Arizona Rivers & Streams Guide	A description of Arizona's most outstanding waterways along with special features and recreational opportunities	8.95		
Access Arizona	Travel guide for disabled and mature travelers	5.00		
Arizona Wildlife Viewing Guide	Maps/markers and Viewing Information for 90 sites	5.95		
Arizona Travel Map	Features all of the state's major roads, attractions, land forms, maps of major cities, and a listing of points of interest	2.25		
Arizona State Trail System Guides, Gold edition				
Guide #1, Trails of Southwestern Arizona	Central and Southwest Deserts: Phoenix, Tucson, Yuma, Central Colorado River areas	8.00		
Guide #2, Trails of Northern Arizona	Canyons, Mesas, Central Highlands: Kaibab National Forest, Grand Canyon, Four Corners areas, Flagstaff	10.00		
Guide #3, Trails of Eastern Arizona	Mogollon Rim, Blue Range, Central East Highlands: Tonto & Apache-Sitgreaves (National Forests)	12.00		
Guide #4, Trails of Southeastern Arizona	Southern Mountain Ranges, River Corridors: Coronado Ntnl. Forest, San Bernardino National Refuge, Catalina Mtns.	10.00		
Arizona State Trail System, Complete Set	Purchase all four guides as a set, and save $5.00!	35.00		
Arizona State Trail System, Supplement to all previous editions	Includes updates for all regions, 48 new trails, 52 revised trails, plus a master index for the third edition	9.00		
Engagement at Picacho Pass	A brief history of Civil War battles which took place at Picacho Peak, and throughout the Southwest.	6.00		

SHIPPING AND HANDLING

Product Total	Add
$6.00 & Under	$3.00
$6.01 - $25.00	$4.00
$25.01 - $75.00	$6.00
$75.01 & Over	$7.00

SUBTOTAL	
SHIPPING	
TAX	(included)
TOTAL	

THANKS FOR YOUR ORDER!
Please allow 4 weeks for delivery.

Make Checks payable to:
Arizona State Parks, Attn: Business Services
1300 W. Washington, Phoenix, AZ 85007

Name: _____
Address: _____
City, State, Zip: _____
Telephone: _____

1300 W. Washington
Phoenix, AZ 85007
Tel & TTY (602) 542-4174
http://www.pr.state.az.us

revised 4/98

WE'LL LEAD YOU TO WATER

"Let the most absent-minded of men be plunged in his deepest reveries—Stand that man on his legs, set his feet a-going, and he will infallibly lead you to water." *Herman Melville's Moby Dick*

As with Melville's absent-minded man, Arizonans' attraction to water borders on the magnetic. A look at the crowds that flock to the state's lakes is a sure way to be convinced of that. But even that impressive army is just a part of the picture. There are legions of other, less visible water worshipers who flock to every river, stream, trickle or pothole no matter how deep in the wilderness it may be hidden. Though that liquid Mecca may amount to little more than a wet streak of sand shaded by a few gnarled cottonwoods, at some time or another you will find it attended by its devotees.

No doubt about it, Arizonans love their water and they love it with a passion honed by the stark dryness of their desert surroundings. This book is designed to serve that love as Melville's absent-minded man might have served it, to get the feet of you water worshippers a-going and lead you to the side of a stream that's exactly the one you're looking for. Whether you want to immerse yourself in a stream and enjoy its coolness or just hike alongside it and watch the wild animals that gather there for sustenance, this book is designed to direct you to water — water that may be less crowded than a marina-lined lake shore, more pleasant than a treeless lake beach. Within these pages you'll find the information you need to make that choice on an informed basis. Once you decide where you want to go, it'll help you get there by the most convenient route possible, and make sure you have a realistic idea of just what to expect when you arrive.

BUT WE WON'T...

Now that you have a rough idea of what this guide is, you should also be made aware of what it isn't. Though these pages include a large amount of very valuable information, they most definitely are not a substitute for a more detailed guide in cases where one is necessary. To make that point more clearly, some streams mentioned here are described as whitewater boating runs. Though the description of these streams contains a rating of their difficulty and though their most serious hazards are identified in the narrative and located on the map, that's still not all you need to know to guarantee a safe trip on any one of them. No guidebook could do that with two brief paragraphs of narrative and a one page schematic map.

So, if you should decide to saddle up your canoe or kayak and set off down one of these streams you would be well advised to first acquire a detailed guide book on that particular run, preferably one that describes it mile by mile. Beyond that, it would also be a good idea to talk

Salome Creek, Dan Dagget

to someone who has already boated the stream and get their impression of it. The reason for doing so is not just to avoid biting off more than you can chew. You may also be saving yourself the trouble of setting off on a run that doesn't measure up to your skill level or your expectations.

Similar advice applies to hikers and anglers who intend to visit some of the more remote stretches of these streams. Before you set off for the backcountry, pick up the appropriate topographic maps as listed in the description and check other guide books for descriptions of the area. You'll probably be very glad you did. Anglers will find it especially valuable to talk to others who may have already fished a stream to learn which stretches are the most productive, among other things. A nearby bait and tackle shop or the regional office of the Arizona Game and Fish Department is usually a good place for such information.

Remember, this book is just a tool to head you in the right direction, not a guide to lead you every step of the way. For more detailed information of that sort you'll have to dig deeper, but at least after reading these pages, you'll know you're digging in the right place.

OF RIVERS THAT FLOW UPSIDE DOWN AND OTHER IMPORTANT FACTS

Now that we've made that disclaimer, we can get on to a fuller description of what actually awaits you within these pages. For one thing, you'll discover some interesting details about Arizona's rivers, like which one is named for its tendency to flow upside down. You'll also learn which one is home to the broadest diversity of hawks, falcons and eagles this side of the National Birds of Prey Area along Idaho's Snake River.

To spare you the suspense, the first is the Hassayampa where, except for along one or two stretches and after an occasional summer monsoon, the sand is on the top and the water on the bottom. The second is a toss-up between Burro Creek near Wickenburg and Eagle Creek near Safford. In each of these areas, you'll find everything from endangered species like peregrine falcons and southern bald eagles to wintering northern bald eagles and Mexican black hawks.

This book will also tell you which of the state's rivers are considered boatable, on a more or less regular basis, and it'll let you in on a new sport that is just being developed to help make that basis even more regular. Appropriately enough, for a region where a stream's boating season can be measured in days or even hours instead of weeks or months, that sport is called low water boating. Using canoes and small inflatables made of slippery and durable plastics that slide over riffles and bounce off rocks, some river runners are finding that they can make their way down streams at levels that in the past have been considered unrunnable. In this way, they are able to extend normally short boating seasons to nearly year-round ones and able to turn streams that traditionally have been considered too small to boat into viable low water runs.

Though navigability is one criterion that qualifies a stream for being included here, it is definitely not the only one. Many of these streams are never boatable, except for an occasional "hair" run by some whitewater daredevil. The reason is, in most cases, that they are too small at low water and too dangerous at high water. The best craft for navigating such waterways is a pair of durable wading sneakers. A few require something a little more complicated, like an air mattress to float your backpack across deep pools that stretch between sheer canyon walls. In a state where the ribbons of green that border its streams serve as such powerful magnets to those who venture beyond the road shoulder, hiking can almost be considered a water sport, one that is just as interesting and just as exciting as boating.

That brings us to reveal what really qualifies a stream for inclusion here, and that is its recreational value. Whether that value is derived from fishing, hiking, birdwatching, or boating, if it is possible for Arizonans to make significant use of a stretch of running water, and if there is nothing blocking their access to it, we included it.

The result is admittedly eclectic. Within these pages you'll find everything from the spectacular 276 miles of the Colorado River that flows through the Grand Canyon, to the one block-long stretch of Granite Creek that provides the city of Prescott with an urban riparian park. To some, that may seem like too broad a range to cover in just one book. However, the purpose of this guide is to be broad, not to be directed toward any one user group or any recreation type.

RIVERS OF DIVERSITY

The best reason for making this guide so wide-ranging is the nature of the subject matter. If one had to pick a single word that describes Arizona's streams, that word would be "diverse." From the East Fork of the Black River high in the White Mountains, to Cave Creek and the Santa Maria of the lower Sonoran Desert, the rivers and streams of Arizona paint a picture of diversity unmatched in any other state. Some flow through alpine meadows lush with wildflowers, while others wander past landscapes almost totally devoid of vegetation. Some roar down deep canyons past sheer walls of solid rock, while others slide through broad, sluggish marshes lined with rushes and cattails.

But the word diversity describes more than just the streams' surroundings. The lush oases these wetways create as they wind their way from mountain to sea are home to one of the most diverse plant and animal communities on the planet. Nearly seventy-five percent of all the wildlife species in Arizona depend on these habitats we refer to as riparian. Here you can see birds like common mergansers, who can barely walk when they're out of water, paddling within a few feet of desert dwelling gila monsters. Moisture loving maiden hair ferns grow in the shadow of cholla cactuses to which water, except in the smallest of quantities, is a deadly poison. The numbers of different types of birds that you may encounter along some of these stretches total into the hundreds.

A FRAGILE BALANCE

All of this broadly branched tree of diversity is balanced precariously on the fragile habitat we call riparian, and a precarious situation it is indeed. Groups like The Nature Conservancy, that are working to protect what is left of our riparian habitat, estimate that up to ninety percent of the lower elevation streamside oases that once crisscrossed the state have already been destroyed. To give cause for even deeper concern, the ten percent that's left is generally in some sort of trouble.

Many of the plant and animal species that once thrived in these areas have become extremely rare. Fish that inhabited streams in numbers so large that they were scooped out of the water in bushel baskets to be used for fertilizer, today exist only in a few remote streams. Some have been reduced to tiny populations in solitary pools that amount to less than the size of a football field. Even the powerful jaguar, which we now think of as a Central and South American species but which once called these gardens of Eden home, now only rarely strays into this historic homeland — even then they never stay.

Much of what has been lost has gone the way of the water that sustained it. Groundwater pumping has reduced streams that once flowed year-round to dry wash storm sewers. Periodically, these sad remnants are wracked by flash floods that sweep away whatever vegetation is left. Other areas have succumbed to overgrazing as well as urban and agricultural development. Streamside trees have even been removed by a thirsty society envious of the moisture they use to stay alive. In other cases too much water has been the problem. Miles of this irreplaceable habitat have been buried under the state's man-made lakes.

WHO ME?

Recreation has played a significant role in this horror story. Remember those crowds we mentioned earlier. Some stretches of stream have been just plain used to death. People roaring around indiscriminately on off-road vehicles, using trees for target practice, hacking at them or breaking off saplings for firewood, strewing trash over the landscape or letting fires get out of control, have all destroyed their share of this rich and irreplaceable resource. If you're the type of visitor who indulges in activities like this, then this book wasn't written for you. It was written for those who are sensitive enough and sensible enough to give this fragile resource the consideration it deserves.

But as much as we like to think it's the slobs that cause all the problems, even conscientious visitors can have negative impacts. Sheer volume can of itself be a destructive force. So what do we do, stay home? No thanks. But we can do our best to minimize the impacts we cause when we do visit these special places.

After years of attempts to educate the public on taking care of the out-of-doors, about the only lesson that seems to have stuck to any significant degree is that one should always make a fire ring at camp. Ironically, that's also the only commandment that has been reconsidered and abandoned. The one thing most people did right is now wrong.

So how do you get people to do things right? Woodsy Owl saying, "Give a hoot don't pollute" hasn't done it. Signs saying "Pack it in/Pack it out" haven't done it. Neither has Clint Eastwood grinding his teeth on those Take Pride in America public service announcements.

How about something simpler than that? How about an easy rule of thumb in which you've already had years of practice learning how to observe and remember? How about just treating the out of doors the way you treat your home? After all, when you're out here, this is your home.

How do you apply this rule of thumb? For one thing, take that empty can you're contemplating throwing into the fire, you wouldn't throw it into your wood stove or fireplace at home, would you? Nor would you chop down the fruit tree in the front yard just to try out your new axe, or blast it with a few shots from your shotgun, or festoon it with fishhooks and monofilament line.

When the need arises out here use the toilet, if there's one available, just as you do at home. It there isn't, bury your waste at least six inches deep, one hundred feet or more from water. On some rivers, boat trips are now required to carry this type of waste out with them. That's going to be the case in more and more places as time goes on, probably even in the more crowded hiking areas. Right now, you can at least carry out your toilet paper. Consider it training.

And there other things you can do to minimize your impact. Don't disturb the wildlife. After all, out here they're your neighbors. And about that fire ring, if there already is one at a campsite when you arrive, you might dig some of the trash out of it. For sure, don't add any. If there isn't any ring, don't build one. It scars the rocks and makes a natural garbage catcher. Just dig a pit for your fire and then fill it in when you get ready to leave.

When you are ready to leave, take a look back at where you've been. How would you feel if you were just arriving? Would you be pleased, or would you have to do a cleanup first? If the latter is the case, you know what to do.

HOW TO USE THIS BOOK

As we said, this book's job is to lead you to water. The best way it can do that, in our opinion, is to get you there without forcing you to dig through complex indexes and long paragraphs of text. For that reason, we've designed this guide to transmit the information quickly and easily. You can learn quite a bit just by thumbing through its pages.

Each stream and river segment that is included is described on just two pages. One page contains written information presented in an easy-to-access format. The facing page contains a map of the stream showing its location in relation to the rest of the state and nearby major cities, as well as special features that you may encounter along its length.

At the top of the text page are a number of headings that tell you at a glance a stream's length, its season, elevation, and the condition of major access routes, as well as any features that might make you want to go to this particular stream and any that might make you consider going elsewhere. Also listed are topographical and other special maps of the area.

Next comes a two paragraph description of those items mentioned under the headings at the top of the page, followed by short, highlighted paragraphs outlining access routes to the stream, nearby facilities, wildlife you might see there, things to watch out for, and sources of further information. At the bottom of the page is a line of symbols called icons that tell you at a glance what recreational activities the stream offers.

Virtually every mark on every page is there to tell you something. Take the tree, bush, and/or cactus that shows up along the blue, curved stream line at the top of every text page. They're not just decorations, they tell you what life-zones the stream flows through. The pine tree is for mountain areas. It can represent either mixed conifer or ponderosa pine habitats. The bush represents the pigmy forest that generally covers intermediate elevations, between highland forests and lowland deserts. In the north, this habitat is made up of grasslands dotted with pinyon and juniper trees. In southern parts of the state it is characterized by scrub oak savannahs.

We picked a saguaro to represent the desert, even though they don't live in many of the state's desert areas. With that in mind, don't expect to find a real saguaro along every stream that has one beside it in this book. Do expect that stream to flow through the desert, however.

In some cases a stream may flow through more than one life-zone — maybe even all three. In that case, more than one symbol will grow along its stream line.

Just below that line you'll find these at-a-glance headings.

LENGTH refers to the distance from beginning to end of the segment described in the narrative and shown on the map. In many cases this information is approximate, at best. Take that into consideration when planning your outing.

SEASON is a bit more complicated. If a stream has a significant annual boating season in the traditional sense, i. e., having enough water to float rafts and kayaks, that's what is listed here. Actually, in many cases this is just an approximation. Every stream in Arizona that has a river running season, except the Colorado River, has an unpredictable one. In a given year, it's possible for any of them not to have a big water boating season at all. We have listed what usually happens, with no guarantee that it will happen the year you go there. To get timely information on any of these streams, get in touch with one of the organizations or agencies listed at the bottom of the page under the heading entitled "INFORMATION" or in the corresponding appendix.

If the stream doesn't have a big water boating season, we tell you if its flow is perennial or intermittent. That's because, in most cases, it's more fun to visit a stream with water in it, even a little water, than a dry wash.

Actually, as we write this guide, there is a bit of a revolution in river running going on in the state that makes it hard to give definitive information under this heading. As we mentioned earlier, boaters who aren't content to resign themselves to a few days of fun per year on most of the state's rivers have started using durable plastic canoes and single person inflatables to run them at levels well below what in the past has been considered boatable. These seemingly stubborn individuals may end up dragging their boats over a riffle too shallow to float once in a while, but to pay that small inconvenience for the reward of a day on the river is well worth it in their eyes. This new sport is even attracting some people who would never have considered canoeing these streams at full flow.

Since the limits of low water boating opportunities afforded by many rivers in the state is still being explored, we can't give you a season for this activity. Instead, if the low water boating icon is "lit," it will indicate that this is a low water boating stream. However, you have to pursue more local information to determine the best time to show up there with your craft.

ACCESS lists the general condition of major access routes to a stream segment. We tell you if the route that leads you there is a paved or a dirt road or a hiking trail, as occasionally is the case. The upstream access is usually listed first. If either route requires a high clearance vehicle (HCV) or four wheel drive (4WD), that is noted here and described under the "CAUTION" heading farther down the page.

ELEVATION gives the distance above sea level of the beginning and end of each stream segment. You can use this information to learn something about the climate along a stream, especially if you take into account the bush or cactus beside the streamline at the top of the page. Generally, the higher an area is, the cooler it will be. At comparable altitudes, however, a desert is warmer than a pinyon-juniper forest, which is warmer than a pine forest.

FEATURES tells you at a glance the reasons you might choose to visit this stream. That may include everything from spectacular scenery to the opportunity to see a particularly rare bird; from exceptionally good fishing to the opportunity to visit an area remote enough to be called a wilderness. In recognition of the fact that one person's delight may be another's dismay, some items may show up in both this category and the next one.

CAUTIONS lists factors that might make you consider going somewhere other than the stream being described. Here you'll read about hazards like unrunnable waterfalls and extremely remote conditions, along with other, less hair raising items like summer heat, crowded conditions, and legal restrictions.

Under this heading, you'll have your first (and, we hope, only) encounter with those ultimate bugaboos of all river runners — strainers. If that name only conjures up visions of wire-screen kitchen utensils, we'd better tell you that a strainer on a stream is a logjam or pile of debris that permits the passage of water, but serves as an impenetrable barrier to boats and boaters. Although these hazards look a lot less impressive than the rocks and waves of big whitewater, they are much more dangerous. If you're unfortunate enough to have a run-in with one of these monsters, your boat or tube will most likely flip over and you and it will be plastered up against the logs, barbed wire, old cars, or whatever happens to form the blockage, by the water rushing through it. In some cases this arrangement lasts until the water goes down or until someone hauls your carcass off the debris pile.

Strainers are most serious on small streams at very high flow levels; when waters rise above stream banks into nearby trees and heavy debris deposited by the most powerful floods. Under these conditions, strainers should be considered a sufficient reason to go elsewhere.

MAPS has two subheadings. The first (**USGS**) lists all the topographical maps covering the area through which the stream segment flows. The second identifies special maps put out by administrative bodies that have jurisdiction over the area. U.S. National Forests (**USFS**), U.S. Bureau of Land Management (**USBLM** or just **BLM**), lands are a couple of examples. In most cases, the topographical maps referred to are standard 1:24,000 scale. In cases where the stream segment covers an exceptionally large area, 1:100,000 scale maps are listed. National Forests and National Parks have exceptionally good maps available of lands they administer. Regrettably, that's not the case for Bureau of Land Management lands and those under state or private ownership.

THE NARRATIVE

In the middle of the page, two paragraphs provide a narrative description of the stream and the area surrounding it. The purpose here is to give you a "feel" for what it's like to actually visit this place. To do that, in most cases we've expanded on items listed under the FEATURES heading at the top of the page, but we also use this part of the description to bring up new items of interest that may give you additional reason to visit the stream. Wildlife, scenery, and cultural sites are a few examples. When it's especially important, we may use this space to give you a more in-depth description of an item mentioned under the CAUTIONS heading.

Another valuable category of information that is frequently expanded upon in the narrative is ACCESS. Occasionally, getting to a stream involves more than just driving down a road and following the signs. In those cases, we try to act like a friendly local, standing by the road giving you on-the-spot directions.

In some instances, the narrative section has been used to briefly describe upstream or downstream segments that didn't get included on their own, but whose description helps fill out the picture of the segment that is included. For those streams that have so many items of interest that it's very hard to mention all of them on one short page, this section provides an opportunity to use a metaphor to describe an area that is otherwise undescribable. The Grand Canyon is one that comes to mind.

ACCESS: Major routes leading to the stream are described in detail here. The upstream access is given first, except in those cases where the upper stretches of a stream may be reached only by hiking from a downstream point.

In cases where access points are very remote or are only used by people visiting the river, directions may be quite sketchy. In those cases, before you set out, it's a good idea to get more detailed directions from a local resident or someone who has been to the river. For obscure access points on navigable rivers, whitewater boating clubs are a good source of information. Anglers and the stores that cater to them are a good bet for all streams.

Some abbreviations you'll run across under this heading and what they stand for include: US=federal highways, AZ=Arizona State Highways, FR=US Forest Service Road, RR=Tribal Reservation Road.

The Streambed Law: In 1987 the Arizona Legislature passed a law making it possible for property owners to take possession of streambed land which until then had belonged to the state. Recreationists were concerned that the new legislation would make many of the state's navigable waterways off-limits to them. To address those concerns, a provision was included in this law that guarantees access to navigable streams as long as those involved are in a boat or something that floats. It also guarantees passage around obstructions that block passage down those waterways even if that passage requires sensible and prudent use of adjacent private lands.

On the other hand, the streambed law does not grant an easement across private property to get to a stream, nor does it grant passage down a river to someone who is not in a boat.

FACILITIES: The first item that gets mentioned under this heading is the availability of nearby campgrounds. Although it is permissible to camp almost anywhere on most public lands, we have called something a campground only if it has obviously been used for that purpose. It's a developed campground if it has picnic tables, pull-in parking places, and toilets. Usually, but not always, these campgrounds have drinking water.

Commercial campgrounds are privately owned and in most cases have electrical hookups. Primitive ones may be no more than a parking place and a fire ring. In many instances, we have said that "other facilities" are available in nearby towns. "Other facilities" in this case refers to restaurants, gas stations, grocery stores, and motels. Don't take it to mean you can always find a campground there. Surprisingly enough, there are towns without campgrounds even in tourist-conscious Arizona.

On multi-day float trips or backpacking trips, you can usually tent-camp by the riverside or along the trail. In areas where that is not the case, we have told you so. For instance, an area along a stretch of a stream might be closed to camping or even closed to all use except river running because there is an eagle nest in the area.

Though a lot of the land on Arizona's Indian reservations looks very much like public land that is open to camping, that is not the case. On tribal lands you can assume that you are only permitted to camp in designated campgrounds and that a tribal permit is required to do so.

WILDLIFE: One of the main reasons people visit streams and streamside areas is to enjoy the wide variety of wild animals that can be seen there. We have tried to list the animals that frequent an area that would be of the broadest interest to the most people. At the same time, we've tried to list animals whose presence tells you something about the area itself. If we say a stream is a good place to see songbirds, you can expect it to support a healthy riparian habitat. If we mention mountain lions, you can bet the area it flows through is quite remote. Spotted owls and black bears mostly live in forested canyons, and so on.

In this section we will usually tell you of any threatened or endangered (T&E) species that live in an area. However, some areas include so many of these rare animals, ranging from birds to fishes to mammals, that there isn't room on one short page to list all of them unless we leave out other species of interest. In those cases we've tried to let variety and interest be our guide while not neglecting T&E species of special note.

One word you'll be running across a lot in this section is "raptors." A raptor is a bird of prey; a hawk, eagle, owl or vulture. Arizona has one of the most diverse raptor populations of any state, and the best place to see these impressive birds, in many cases, is along the state's streams.

CAUTIONS: Here, we give you a detailed description of any hazards you need to be warned about on a stream segment. Also mentioned under this heading are regulations you need to obey that are directly related to the stream and its use, any permits you'll need, and any measures you'll have to take care of in advance to ensure a safe, hassle free trip.

If there is something in the area that may cause you inconvenience, such as confusing jurisdictional overlaps between government agencies, we warn you about that. In cases where it is appropriate, we caution you to show respect for local residents, their customs, and their private property.

Again, you should not consider this an exhaustive list of troublesome areas along a stream or hassles you may encounter there. Use it as a reason to inquire further.

INFORMATION: Under this heading we list those organizations or agencies that are a source of further information about the stream. In most cases, this includes a national forest ranger district or a BLM district office. Other possibilities are national park headquarters, state government offices, and Native American tribal offices. Sometimes a local chamber of commerce is mentioned.

We do not list groups here that are understood to be good sources on all or nearly all rivers in the state. Some of those are the Northern or Central Arizona Paddlers Clubs, Trout Unlimited, and the National Audubon Society. They are listed in the appendix entitled "Information Sources." Valuable information on facilities may be available from chambers of commerce of towns near stream segments, even though they are not mentioned under this heading.

USES: At the bottom of each descriptive page there is a row of seven symbols called icons. Each of them represents a recreational activity covered by this guide. They make it possible to key-in on all the streams that offer a particular recreational opportunity with a flick of your thumb.

Of these seven icons, six are standards that are on every descriptive page in this book. These include boating, low water boating, waterplay, fishing, hiking, and camping. The seventh is a "wild card" — one that can be used to point out an activity that is especially notable along the stretch of stream being considered. Some segments have no wild cards. The most any segment can have is one.

If an icon is "lit," by which we mean printed in bold black, you know the activity designated is available on that stream segment. If the symbol is a shadowy gray, that activity is unavailable, or at best marginally available, along that segment.

This handy section goes beyond telling you just whether or not a recreation is possible on a stream. Where it's appropriate, additional information relevant to that activity is printed under its symbol. For instance, if the fishing icon is lit, underneath it will be the type of fishing (warm or cold water) of predominant interest along that stretch of stream.

The boating icon goes a step further. It is the only one that may change form from stream to stream. If a stream segment requires whitewater equipment and skills, the boating icon will be lit and will show a whitewater kayak. Under it will be listed the difficulty rating of the stream on the international 1-6 scale with 6 being the most difficult (life-threatening). If the segment is flat water, the icon will show a rowboat without a difficulty rating.

Other descriptive notes on the icons are shown on the "Icon Key" page (page 14).

THE MAPS

Facing each descriptive page is a map. As with the text, the maps we have included are abbreviated and designed to communicate valuable but limited information quickly and efficiently. They show you where a stream segment is located in relation to the rest of the state and how its location relates to large population centers and highways.

The main purpose of these shorthand maps is to show you how to get to a stream and to give you an idea of the location of some major points of interest along it. The location of nearby facilities, like campgrounds and picnic areas, is also noted.

As we have said before, these maps are not intended to be used as a substitute for a detailed whitewater boating guide or as a hiking guide to any stream. If you plan to boat one of these waterways or hike along it, pick up a whitewater guide book, if one is available, and/or acquire the appropriate topographic maps listed at the top of the page.

Other descriptive notes on the maps are shown on the "Map Key" page (page 15).

SO, WHAT ARE YOU WAITING FOR?

By now, if we're doing our job right, your feet are ready to get going to some cottonwood-lined stream or other. Don't let us hold you up. Dive into the text and pick out one that suits your fancy.

One of the reasons the Arizona State Parks Board commissioned this book was to take pressure off the more crowded lake side recreation sites around the state and spread the user load around a bit. Some of you will reap the benefits in less crowded recreation areas. Others will grumble that this guide is just going to bring more people to their once secluded hangouts. Hopefully, the positives will balance or even outweigh the negatives. The best chance of that being the case is if those of you who do visit our state's streams do so with the feeling of respect and affection that they deserve.

One benefit which may accrue from any added interest that this book inspires is that, as more people come to know Arizona's streams and rivers, more will stand up for them when they face pressures that may be detrimental. After all, not even a river can have too many friends when it needs them, and the day of need for Arizona's magnificent oases is most definitely here.

So, head on out to boat those rivers and hike those canyons and learn to love them while you do. Get yourself a canoe if you don't already have one; and set off down some twisting, winding course lined with beaches and shaded with cottonwoods. Our bet is you won't feel cheated when you have to drag it over a riffle or two. We've set you on a hot trail that leads to some of the most beautiful places this side of paradise; the rest is up to you. Just think of all the fun you're going to have when you get there.

THE INTERNATIONAL WHITEWATER RATING SCALE

At the bottom of each page that describes a river with a whitewater boating season, there is a Roman numeral under the whitewater boating icon. This number ranges from I to VI (or 1-6 in more familiar arabic numbers). It rates the river's rapids on a scale of difficulty that has been standardized around the world with VI being the most difficult, and I the easiest. A description of the characteristics of each level of difficulty is as follows:

Class I: Still or moving water with few (if any) riffles or obstructions.

Class II: Small rapids with waves up to 3 feet high and obvious clear channels not requiring scouting.

Class III: Powerful rapids with waves up to 5 feet high. Some maneuvering required to miss obstacles. (Generally speaking, Class III is the upper limit for open canoes.)

Class IV: Long difficult rapids requiring intricate maneuvering in turbulent waters. Scouting often necessary. Rescue difficult.

Class V: Extremely difficult, extremely violent rapids, requiring difficult and precise maneuvering to avoid numerous serious obstacles. Rescue difficult at best, impossible at worst. The Class V designation is reserved for those rapids which only a tiny minority of paddlers can run safely (or at all).

Class VI: The most extreme whitewater. This classification is generally synonymous with unrunnable. (Fletcher Anderson and Ann Hopkins report in **Rivers of the Southwest**, that in Europe it is a common practice to downgrade a rapid from Class VI to Class V if someone succeeds in running it.)

This system was devised to take the subjective element out of rating rivers. Since some mere mortal always has to apply it and another has to interpret it, that lofty goal remains unattained. Still, this system does make a respectable run at it and will probably keep most people from showing up at the Grand Canyon with a rubber dinghy. Just remember, it's better to err on the safe side.

ICONS

 Whitewater boating

 No big water boating

 Flat water boating

 Low water boating

 No low water boating

 Waterplay

 No waterplay

 Fishing

 No or poor fishing

 Hiking trails

 No hiking trails

 Undeveloped camping

 No camping

 Developed camping

Wildcard ICONS

 Birdwatching

 Wild animals commonly sighted

 Picnicking

 Photography/spectacular scenery

 Horseback riding

 An area with historical or archaeological significance

 Power boating

Map Symbols

Divided Highway and Freeways

Paved Road, suitable for all cars

Dirt or Gravel Road, inquire about conditions

Stream Segment

Other Streams

Trail

➤ Arrows show location of segment and point down stream

State Border

Special Use Areas, i.e., Closed or Restricted Entry

Agency Jurisdictional Boundaries
   i.e., Forest Service, Indian lands, Wilderness

P Parking Areas

▲ Campgrounds

◎ ○ Cities and Towns

□ Sites of Special Interest

60 Interstate Highway

60 U.S. Highway

Y70 Reservation Route

60 State Highway

North is always
towards the
top of the page

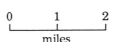

miles

The scale will
change from
map to map

	White River Boating	Flat Water Boating	Power boating	Low Water boating	Cold Water Fishing	Warm Water Fishing	Waterplay	Developed camping	Undeveloped camping	Hiking	Birdwatching	Wildlife	Horseback riding	Photography	Picnicking	History/Archaeology	Page Number
Northern Rivers and Streams																	
Canyon de Chelly										●	●					●	20
Chevelon Creek					●	●				●	●			●			22
Colorado River - Glen Canyon			●			●		●		●	●	●					24
Colorado River - Grand Canyon	●								●	●	●		●	●		●	26
Colorado River - Western G. C.	●		●						●		●		●				28
East Clear Creek					●	●				●	●			●			30
Havasu Creek							●			●	●			●			32
Little Colorado - Headwaters					●	●				●	●		●		●		34
Little Colorado - Grand Falls		●					●			●					●	●	36
Little Colorado - Cameron							●			●			●		●	●	38
Paria River							●			●	●		●		●		40
Virgin River					●		●			●	●		●	●			42
Western Rivers and Streams																	
Bill Williams River							●			●	●			●			46
Burro Creek					●					●	●			●			48
Colorado River - Black Canyon			●				●	●	●	●	●		●				50
Colorado River - Topock Gorge			●	●			●	●	●		●		●				52
Colorado River - Parker Dam			●	●	●	●	●	●	●					●			54
Colorado River - Ehrenberg			●	●			●	●	●		●		●				56
Colorado River - Laguna Dam			●	●		●	●	●	●			●					58
Santa Maria River										●		●	●				60
Southern Rivers and Streams																	
Aravaipa Creek							●			●		●	●				64
Cave Creek - Chiricahuas							●			●	●	●		●			66
Cienega Creek							●			●		●				●	68
Gardner Canyon (Upper Cienega)							●			●		●		●			70
Hot Springs Canyon							●			●		●	●			●	72
Madera Canyon							●			●	●	●		●			74
Redfield Canyon							●			●		●		●			76
Sabino Canyon							●			●		●	●				78
San Pedro River							●	●		●	●	●	●	●		●	80
Sonoita Creek							●			●		●	●				82
Sycamore Creek							●			●		●	●				84
Eastern Rivers and Streams																	
Big Bonita Creek						●	●			●		●	●				88
Black River - East Fork						●	●		●	●				●			90
Black River - West Fork						●	●			●		●		●			92
Black River - Reservation						●	●			●		●		●			94

A GLANCE

	White River Boating	Flat Water Boating	Power boating	Low Water Boating	Waterplay	Cold Water Fishing	Warm Water Fishing	Hiking	Developed camping	Undeveloped camping	Birdwatching	Wildlife	Picnicking	Photography	Horseback riding	History/Archaeology	Page Number
Blue River	●				●	●		●		●	●						96
Bonita Creek					●			●		●	●						98
Canyon Creek					●	●		●		●				●			100
Cherry Creek					●			●		●						●	102
Cibeque Creek					●	●		●		●				●			104
Eagle Creek					●	●		●	●		●						106
Gila River - US 666 Bridge	●			●	●			●		●	●						108
Gila River - Coolidge Dam					●		●	●	●		●						110
Gila River - Kelvin	●			●	●		●			●						●	112
Salt River - US 60	●			●	●		●	●		●		●					114
Salt River - Gleason Flats	●			●	●		●	●				●					116
Salt River - Horsehoe Bend	●			●	●		●	●			●						118
Salt River - Stewart Mtn Dam	●				●		●			●	●						120
San Francisco River - Hot Spgs	●			●	●		●	●		●	●						122
San Francisco River - Clifton	●			●	●		●	●		●	●						124
White River - North Fork					●	●		●	●			●					126
White River - East Fork					●	●		●		●	●						128
Central Rivers and Streams																	
Agua Fria River					●			●		●	●					●	132
Cave Creek - (Seven Springs)					●			●	●		●						134
East Verde River					●	●		●	●		●						136
Fossil Creek					●			●		●	●						138
Granite Creek					●			●		●	●						140
Hassayampa River					●			●			●						142
Oak Creek - Pumphouse					●	●		●	●		●						144
Oak Creek - Sedona				●			●	●	●				●				146
Salome Creek					●	●		●	●			●					148
Sycamore Creek					●			●		●			●				150
Tonto Creek - Fish Hatchery					●	●		●	●			●					152
Tonto Creek - Gisela	●				●	●		●		●	●						154
Tonto Creek - Rye Creek					●						●						156
Verde River - Perkinsville	●			●			●	●			●						158
Verde River - Clarkdale	●			●	●	●	●	●		●			●				160
Verde River - Camp Verde	●			●	●	●	●			●	●						162
Verde River - Beasley Flats	●			●	●		●	●		●	●						164
Verde River - Childs	●			●	●		●	●		●	●						166
Verde River - Horseshoe Dam	●			●	●		●	●		●	●						168
Verde River - Bartlett Dam	●			●	●		●	●		●	●						170
West Clear Creek				●	●	●		●		●	●						172
Wet Beaver Creek				●	●	●		●		●	●						174

Arizona Rivers and Streams Guide

Northern Section

Canyon de Chelly
Chevelon Creek
Colorado River
East Clear Creek
Havasu Creek
Little Colorado River
Paria River
Virgin River

Grand Canyon, by Kenneth Walters

CANYON DE CHELLY

LENGTH: **20.8 miles**   SEASON: **Perennial flow**
ACCESS: **Paved road**   ELEVATION: **7500' - 5515'**
FEATURES: **Ancient ruins, superb scenery, guided tours**
CAUTIONS: **Restricted access, private property**
MAPS: **USGS -** Canyon de Chelly (1:100,000) or Canyon del Muerto (15')
       USNPS - Canyon de Chelly National Monument

C anyon de Chelly and nearby Canyon del Muerto contain some of the best preserved prehistoric Indian ruins in the southwest. Even though this is a national monument, all of the land is privately owned by the Navajo Tribe. Access is limited to guided tours to preserve the privacy of the residents. Most visitors just drive the rim and enjoy the view from a distance, but for a closer look, the 1.25 mile trail to White House Ruin is open to unescorted hikers.

Other access is provided by horse rides or jeep tours along the canyon floor. One of these trips can provide a memorable glimpse into the Navajos' lifestyle as well as a close-up look at the ruins.

ACCESS: At the I-40, Chambers exit (East of Flagstaff) drive north on US 191 to Chinle then east to the National Monument. The trailhead to White House Ruin is located about six miles from the visitor center along the south rim drive.

FACILITIES: Guide services are located at the visitor center. Camping, lodging and food are available at the monument entrance. Other facilities are available in Chinle.

WILDLIFE: This area is heavily farmed by the Navajo. Except for riparian birds, you are more likely to see domestic sheep than wild animals.

CAUTIONS: Access to any area but White House Ruin Trail requires a guide. This is a residential area. Please respect residents' privacy.

INFORMATION: Canyon de Chelly National Monument; Navajo Tribe

USES:

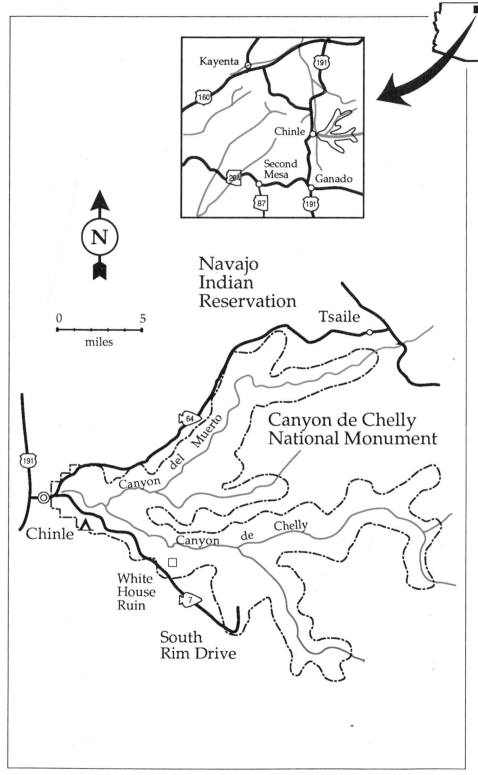

Kayenta

191

160

Chinle

Second
Mesa

264

Ganado

87

191

N

0   5
miles

Navajo
Indian
Reservation

Tsaile

64

Canyon del Muerto

Canyon de Chelly
National Monument

191

Canyon

Chinle

Canyon   de   Chelly

White
House
Ruin

7

South
Rim Drive

CHEVELON CREEK

LENGTH: **34 miles**　　　　　SEASON: **Perennial flow**
ACCESS: **Dirt road, hiking trail**　　ELEVATION: **7500′ - 4900′**
FEATURES: **Forested canyon, trout fishing, cool summers**
CAUTIONS: **Limited access, remote area**
MAPS: **USGS** - Woods Canyon, Porcupine Ridge, Weimer Point, Chevelon
　　　　Crossing, Potato Wash North, Relic Point, McCauley Sinks, Hibbard
　　　　USFS- Apache-Sitgreaves National Forest

F ishing is the main reason people come here, but hiking and water play
also serve as strong incentives. This little stream flows through a steep,
narrow gorge as it crawls down the back of the Mogollon Rim on its
way to join the Little Colorado. Mixed conifers cling to canyon slopes and
mingle with riparian species along the streambed. In the upper reaches,
large brown trout lurk in shaded pools to lure anglers and test their skills.
Most people gain access by hiking down from Woods Canyon Lake.

About halfway through the National Forest the stream is held back by
a dam that forms Chevelon Lake. Below the dam, fishing is best in the
spring when the stream is regularly stocked with trout. Plentiful wildlife is
another reason to come here. There are birds to watch and perhaps a bear to
see as it forages along the forested slopes of the canyon.

ACCESS: Drive east out of Payson
on AZ 260 to FR 300 (Woods Canyon Lake Road). Hike downstream
from the dam into Woods Canyon
and on to Chevelon Canyon. Or
continue past Woods Canyon Lake
on FR 300 and turn north on FR 169
at Alder Lake to Chevelon Lake. FR
169 also continues on to Chevelon
Crossing which affords access to the
lower portions of the stream.

FACILITIES: There are USFS
developed campgrounds at Woods
Canyon Lake, Chevelon Lake and
Chevelon Crossing. Nearest other
facilities are in Payson.

WILDLIFE: Woodland birds mix
with migratory warblers. There's a
chance you could see a spotted owl
here, recently declared a threatened
species. The area hosts a number of
whitetail deer, rarer in the west than
their mule deer cousins.

CAUTIONS: The area within the
canyon is quite remote, especially if
you venture very far. More accessible areas can become quite
crowded during peak use times.

INFORMATION: Apache-Sitgreaves National Forest, Chevelon
Ranger District

USES:

cold　　　　　　　fee

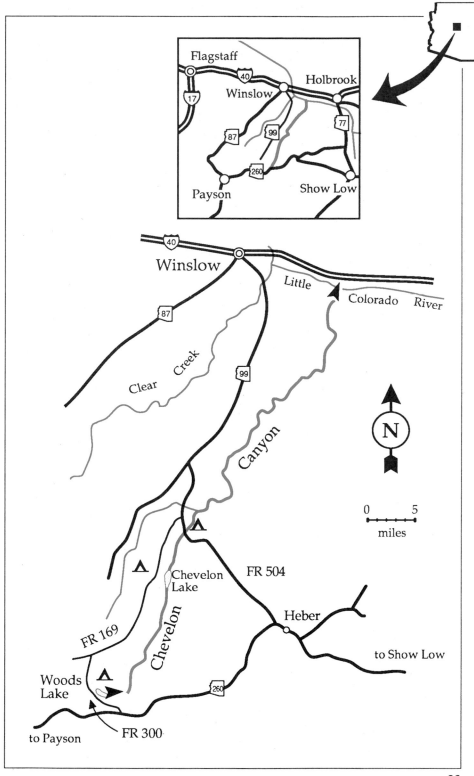

COLORADO RIVER — Glen Canyon

LENGTH: **15.5 miles**
ACCESS: **Paved road**
SEASON: **All year**
ELEVATION: **3200' - 3116'**
FEATURES: **Blue ribbon trout stream, scenic canyon**
CAUTIONS: **No access at Glen Canyon Dam, cold water**
MAPS: **USGS** - Page, Ferry Swale, Lees Ferry
      USNPS - Glen Canyon National Recreation Area

T his short stretch of the Colorado River is reminiscent of Glen Canyon prior to construction of the dam. The rest of its narrow side canyons, ancient Indian ruins and placid meanders are buried beneath Lake Powell. The warm, muddy waters that once flowed here are now clear and cold as they gush from the depths of Lake Powell. As a result, the river teems with trout instead of Colorado squawfish and razorback suckers. However, that change meets with the enthusiastic approval of the many fishermen who come here to try for a record-size catch.

Access for boaters is at Lees Ferry only, from which it is possible to motor all the way to Glen Canyon Dam. If you head downstream of Lees Ferry, you are committed to run 226 miles of rapids in the Grand Canyon, for which you need a permit and an appropriate whitewater boat.

ACCESS: <u>Lees Ferry</u>: Take US 89 north 111 miles from Flagstaff to US 89A, then 14 miles to the Lees Ferry turnoff. <u>Glen Canyon Dam</u>: Take US 89 north from Flagstaff 137 miles.

FACILITIES: There is a boat ramp, campground, and picnic area at Lees Ferry. Other facilities are available nearby along US 89A and in Page.

WILDLIFE: Some of the largest rainbow trout in the lower forty-eight states inhabit the waters of this stretch of river.

CAUTIONS: Fishing boats go upstream of Lees Ferry only. Downstream there are dangerous rapids and no exit for 226 miles. The water here is too cold for swimming.

INFORMATION: Visitor's center at Glen Canyon National Recreation Area. Research and dam operations only at Bureau of Reclamation Grand Canyon Monitoring and Research Center.

USES:

                        cold   fee

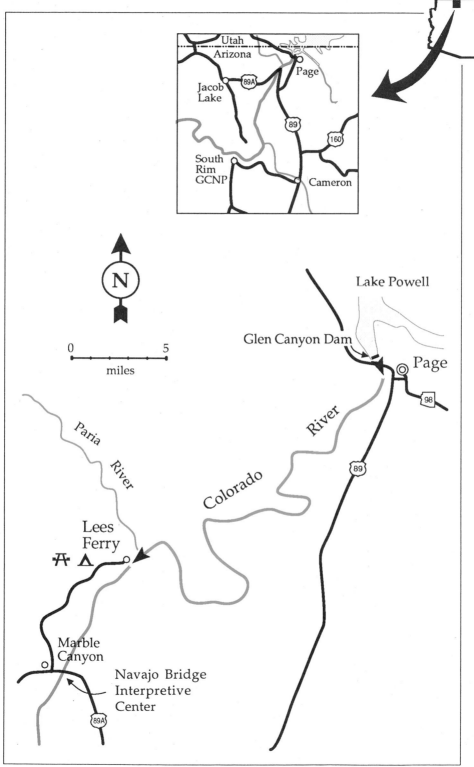

Utah
Arizona

Page

89A

Jacob
Lake

89

160

South
Rim
GCNP

Cameron

N

0   5
miles

Lake Powell

Glen Canyon Dam

Page

98

Paria

River

River

Colorado

89

Lees
Ferry

Marble
Canyon

Navajo Bridge
Interpretive
Center

89A

COLORADO RIVER—Grand Canyon

LENGTH: **225.5 miles** SEASON: **All year**
ACCESS: **Paved road/dirt road (HCV)** ELEVATION: **3140' - 1360'**
FEATURES: **Unmatched scenery, exciting rapids, unforgettable adventure**
CAUTIONS: **Big rapids, long distances, remote setting**
MAPS: **USGS -** (1:100,000) Peach Springs, Mt. Trumbull, Grand Canyon,
 Tuba City, Glen Canyon Dam
 USNPS - Grand Canyon National Park

Running the Colorado River through the Grand Canyon is one of the premier outdoor experiences available to relatively large numbers of people. Every year 22,000 individuals pay to shoot rapids like Lava Falls and Sockdolager. But there's more to the Grand Canyon than rapids. The scenery is unforgettable — especially in side canyons like Elves Chasm, Havasu Creek, and Kanab Canyon. In addition, the hiking trails are breathtaking and the photo opportunities are sensational.

For some, a trip through this mile-deep gorge provides the adventure of a lifetime, others come back again and again for a lifetime of adventure. For more detailed information, read some of the dozens of fine books that have been written about 'The Canyon.' Or better, go see it for yourself.

ACCESS: (From Flagstaff) <u>Lees Ferry</u>: Take US 89 north 111 miles, then US 89A for 14 miles, to the Lees Ferry turnoff. <u>Diamond Creek</u>: Take I-40 to Seligman, then US 66 to Peach Springs. A permit is required to enter the Hualapai Reservation and drive the 25 miles to the river. A number of hiking trails lead to the river from both rims.

FACILITIES: There is a developed campground and boat ramp at Lees Ferry and commercial facilities nearby along US 89A. Phantom Ranch, at river mile 88, offers a few facilities. No facilities at the take-out.

WILDLIFE: Endangered peregrine falcon, rare desert bighorn sheep, and the shy Grand Canyon rattlesnake are just some of the fascinating creatures you may encounter here. Trout fishing is excellent for the first half of the run.

CAUTIONS: A permit is required for river trips and overnight camping. The current is strong and the water is cold. People have been killed by being swept into the rapids. Wading without a life jacket is dangerous, swimming without one can be fatal.

INFORMATION: Grand Canyon National Park; Hualapai Tribe

USES:

class III-V cold

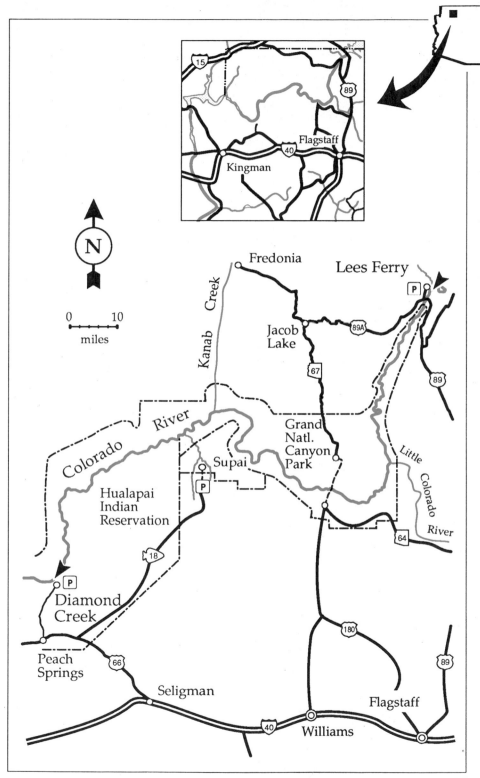

COLORADO RIVER — Western Grand Canyon

LENGTH: **54 miles** SEASON: **All year**
ACCESS: **Dirt road (HCV)** ELEVATION: **1360' - 1200'**
FEATURES: **Spectacular scenery , whitewater, interesting hikes**
CAUTIONS: **Strong currents, cold water, rugged access**
MAPS: **USGS -** (1:100,000) Mt. Trumbull, Peach Springs
  USNPS - Grand Canyon National Park

Most Grand Canyon River trips take out at Diamond Creek. However, those who want to see all of the Grand Canyon continue on to Pierce Ferry in the upper reaches of Lake Mead. Here the rapids are still exciting, the hiking is just as interesting, and the scenery remains breathtaking.

When Major John Wesley Powell first boated through the Grand Canyon, three of his crew deserted above one particularly bad rapid here. They hiked out through what is now called Separation Canyon and were never seen again. The point of their desertion now marks the beginning of Lake Mead. Power boaters regularly venture into these lower reaches of the Canyon to fish and sightsee.

ACCESS: <u>Diamond Creek</u>: Take I-40 west from Flagstaff to Seligman, then US 66 to Peach Springs. A permit is required to enter the Hualapai Reservation and drive the 25 miles to the river. <u>Pierce Ferry</u>: Take US 93 north from Kingman, 27 miles to the Meadview turnoff, then 48 miles to Pierce Ferry.

FACILITIES: There is a primitive campground at Pierce Ferry. Gas and a convenience store are available in Meadview. Other facilities in Kingman and Seligman.

WILDLIFE: Desert bighorn sheep, once a threatened species, are some-times seen along this stretch. Some very large striped bass have been caught at the head of Lake Mead.

CAUTIONS: Even though the rapids here are not as big as those above Diamond Creek, they are still worthy of respect. Lake Mead can be very windy: some trips use motors. A permit from the Hualapai Tribe is required to enter their reservation. Permits are required to run the river, one from the tribe and one from Grand Canyon National Park.

INFORMATION: Grand Canyon National Park; Hualapai Tribe; Lake Mead National Recreation Area

USES:

Class III-IV warm

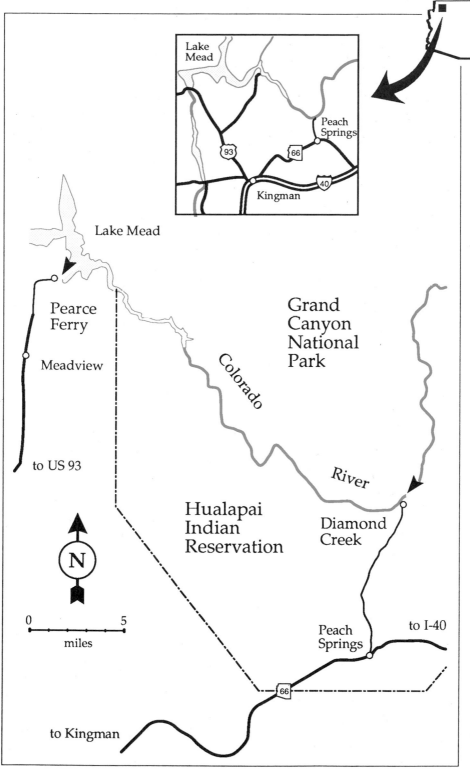

North

Lake Mead

Peach Springs

93

66

40

Kingman

Lake Mead

Pearce Ferry

Meadview

Grand Canyon National Park

Colorado

to US 93

River

Hualapai Indian Reservation

Diamond Creek

N

0   5

miles

Peach Springs

to I-40

66

to Kingman

EAST CLEAR CREEK

LENGTH: **31 miles** SEASON: **Perennial flow**
ACCESS: **Dirt road, hiking trail** ELEVATION: 6500' - 4900'
FEATURES: **Scenic vistas, trout fishing, beautiful canyon**
CAUTIONS: **Limited access, remote area, rattlesnakes**
MAPS: **USGS** - Blue Ridge Reservoir, Leonard Canyon, Quayle Hill,
   Hamilton Crossing
   USFS - Coconino National Forest

T he rocky, secluded canyon through which this little stream flows makes
it a popular place with backcountry hikers and backpackers. The high
canyon walls resemble those of West Clear Creek just over the rim, but
of the two canyons, this is the more accessible. A number of hiking trails
lead to remote areas along the stream where you might see a black bear, a
coatimundi, or even a rare spotted owl. If you walk along the bottom of the
canyon expect to wade, but probably not to swim.

The stream holds some resident rainbow and brown trout as well as a
few native Apache trout. Fishing is best in the spring when there's plenty of
water. The trout are wild, not stocked. One of the most popular access
points is along FR 95 from which you can hike and fish either up or downstream. The Horse Crossing and Kinder Crossing trails provide other routes
into this scenic, remote area.

ACCESS: From Payson drive north
on AZ 87 through Pine to the Blue
Ridge Ranger Station. Turn south on
FR 95 and drive approximately 6
miles to the creek. Four miles from
AZ 87, FR 513B heads north to
Horse Crossing Trail and FR 19
heads east to Kinder Crossing Trail.

FACILITIES: There is a USFS
developed campground at Rock
Crossing at Blue Ridge Reservoir.
Other facilities are available in Clints
Well, Strawberry, Pine and Payson.

WILDLIFE: Rattlesnakes are fairly
plentiful here. The area is consid-

ered possible spotted owl habitat —
they have been seen in nearby
Leonard Canyon. Look for bear,
coatimundi and beavers, bobcat too.
The little bird that flits around just
above the waters of the stream is a
black phoebe.

CAUTIONS: See above for rattlesnakes. The canyon is quite remote
with precipitous cliffs and steep
trails. Don't watch too closely for
those snakes.

INFORMATION: Coconino National Forest, Blue Ridge Ranger Dist

USES:

cold   fee

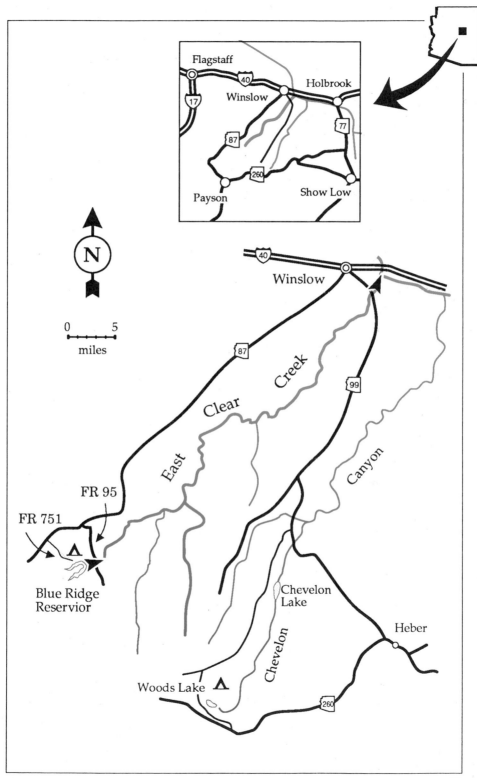

HAVASU CREEK

LENGTH: **9.6 miles**   SEASON: **Perennial flow**
ACCESS: **Hiking/horseback trail**   ELEVATION: **3270' - 1790'**
FEATURES: **Indian village, waterfalls, swimming holes**
CAUTIONS: **Permit required; strenuous hike; hot, dry trail**
MAPS: **USGS** - Grand Canyon (1:100,000)
          USNPS - Grand Canyon National Park

T he canyon through which Havasu Creek flows is one of the most
popular hiking areas within the Grand Canyon. One look at its spectacular waterfalls and inviting swimming holes and you'll know why
so many are willing to hike ten hot, dry miles to come here.

This is the home of the Havasupai Tribe, the only permanent residents
of the Grand Canyon. Their name is descriptive of the stream that is the life-
blood of their culture. It means "people of the blue-green waters." The color
of the creek is so rich that photos of it look almost too vivid to be real.
Naturally dissolved calcium carbonate, the same mineral that forms stalactites and stalagmites in caves and the travertine dams of Havasu creek,
causes the creek to reflect the blue of the sky and take on its unique color.

ACCESS: Turn north off US 66 just east of Peach Springs. The road is paved 60 miles to Hualapai Hilltop trailhead. From there it is an eight mile hike to the village of Supai and the creek, and two more miles to the campground. The trail follows the creek 8 miles farther to the Colorado River.

FACILITIES: There is a parking lot and water at the trailhead. Two miles downstream from the village of Supai is a primitive campground beside the creek. A hotel, hostel, grocery store, and diner are located in Supai.

WILDLIFE: Rare desert bighorn sheep and endangered peregrine falcon can be seen here.

CAUTIONS: Most of this canyon is within the reservation of the Ha-vasupai Tribe. Visitors to the canyon are assessed a fee for entry and an additional one for lodging. Permits should be acquired in advance. The hike in can be extremely hot be-tween May and October.

INFORMATION: Havasupai Tribal Council; Grand Canyon National Park

USES:

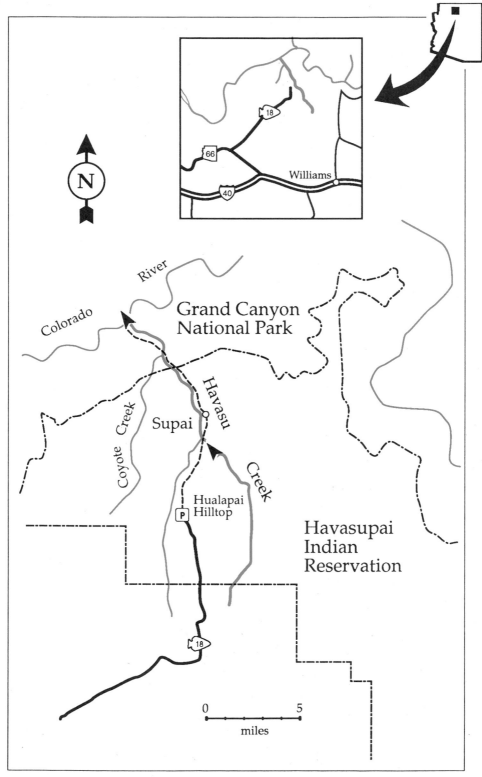

N

18

66

Williams

40

Colorado River

Grand Canyon National Park

Coyote Creek

Supai

Havasu

Creek

Hualapai Hilltop

P

Havasupai Indian Reservation

18

0   5

miles

LITTLE COLORADO RIVER
— Headwaters to Forest Boundary

LENGTH: **18 miles**   SEASON: **Perennial flow**
ACCESS: **Dirt road, hiking trail**   ELEVATION: **9600' - 8000'**
FEATURES: **Scenic vistas, trout fishing, beautiful canyon**
CAUTIONS: **Limited access, remote area**
MAPS: **USGS** - Greens Peak, Greer, Eagar, Springerville
       USFS - Apache-Sitgreaves National Forest

Anyone who only knows the Little Colorado River as the dry wash that passes under I-40 near Winslow wouldn't believe this ribbon of dust could ever be a trout stream. But high along the Mogollon Rim that's exactly what it is. From source to mouth this stream actually varies considerably. In the mountains it exists as a number of alpine brooks or forks, all cool and clear and full of trout. People hike, fish, and camp along them and watch the many different types of wildlife that live there.

Finally, these forks, East, West, South, and Hall Creek, flow together to form the Little Colorado. The stream thus united leaves the mountains to begin its twisting journey through the petrified forest and painted desert. Along the way it passes through an area that boasts some of the heaviest concentrations of ancient cultural sites in the nation. For its last hurrah it takes a spectacular plunge into the Grand Canyon. How's that for diversity?

ACCESS: From Eagar, follow the river 5 miles upstream via AZ 260. Turn south on FR 560 to the South Fork Campground and Trail #97 which offers access. Farther along, AZ 260, AZ 373 and FR 112/113 branch off to the south to points along Hall Creek and the West and East Forks.

FACILITIES: There are USFS developed campgrounds at the South Fork Trailhead, along AZ 373 in the vicinity of Greer, and on FR 554 off FR 113 between the West and East Forks. Other facilities are available in Springerville.

WILDLIFE: This is an excellent area in which to see elk and mule deer. Black bear and wild turkeys are plentiful also. All of the forks contain trout.

CAUTIONS: The inner reaches of some of these canyons are quite remote; be prepared if you venture very far. In some places there are no hiking trails and you will have to walk in the stream bed.

INFORMATION: Apache-Sitgreaves National Forest, Greer Ranger District

USES:

cold   fee

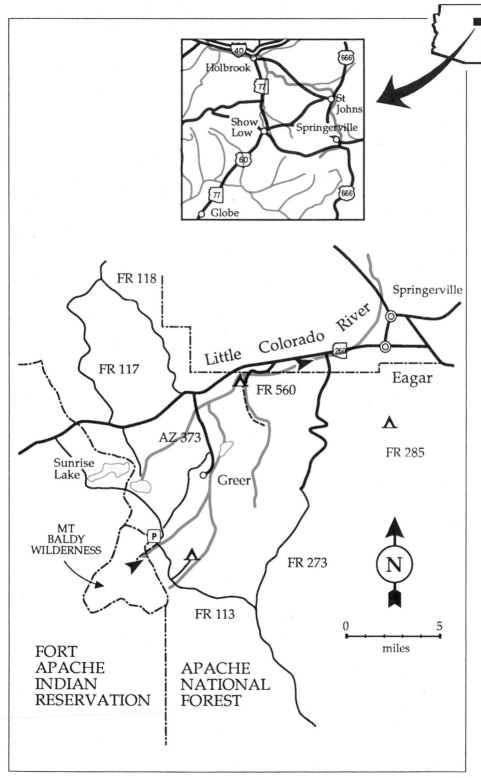

North

FR 118

Springerville

Little Colorado River

Eagar

FR 117

FR 560

AZ 373

FR 285

Sunrise Lake

Greer

MT BALDY WILDERNESS

P

FR 273

FR 113

N

0   5
miles

FORT APACHE INDIAN RESERVATION

APACHE NATIONAL FOREST

Holbrook

St Johns

Show Low

Springerville

Globe

LITTLE COLORADO RIVER
— Grand Falls to Cameron

LENGTH: **40 miles**   SEASON: **Intermittent**
ACCESS: **Dirt road, paved road**   ELEVATION: **4600' - 4000'**
FEATURES: **Spectacular waterfall, scenic canyon, prehistoric ruins**
CAUTIONS: **Indian reservation, permits needed, boating restricted, dam**
MAPS: **USGS** - Grand Falls; Standing Rocks; Wupatki SE and NE; Cameron
       SE, S, and N
       USBIA - Navajo Nation

N orth of Winslow, the river plunges over Grand Falls, a steep escarpment higher than Niagara. When the flow is swollen with spring snow melt or summer monsoons, the spectacle can be impressive.

Most people come here to see the falls and view the surrounding desert. The area is dotted with ruins, especially within Wupatki National Monument. Although the Navajo Nation prohibits boating access below Grand Falls, people have run the river downstream where one bank is privately owned. The rapids are challenging, but navigable by canoes, kayaks and small rafts at moderate levels. Seven or eight miles below the falls the river flattens out again. Near the Wupatki take-out, what was once an old dam has filled with sand and become Black Falls. It is unrunnable.

ACCESS: From Flagstaff drive north on US 89 to the edge of town, east on the Townsend Winona Road for 8 miles, then northeast on the Leupp Road about twelve miles to where the Grand Falls road forks off to the north. Other access is possible at Wupatki National Monument via the Wukoki Road and from the US 89 truck crossing at Cameron.

FACILITIES: Grand Falls has a picnic area. Cameron has a restaurant, motel, and gas station. Commercial campgrounds and other facilities are available in Flagstaff.

WILDLIFE: There is a colony of burrowing owls co-habiting with

some prairie dogs at the Grand Falls turnoff. At the falls you might hear a canyon wren or see herds of Navajo horses on the hills bordering the river.

CAUTIONS: The Navajo Tribe requires permits for all activities on their reservation. No camping is permitted at Grand Falls. Wupatki National Monument asks that you notify them before putting on the river from their lands. *Portage Black Falls* (the old dam) near the Wukoki Road access.

INFORMATION: Navajo Nation; Wupatki National Monument

USES:
Class II-III

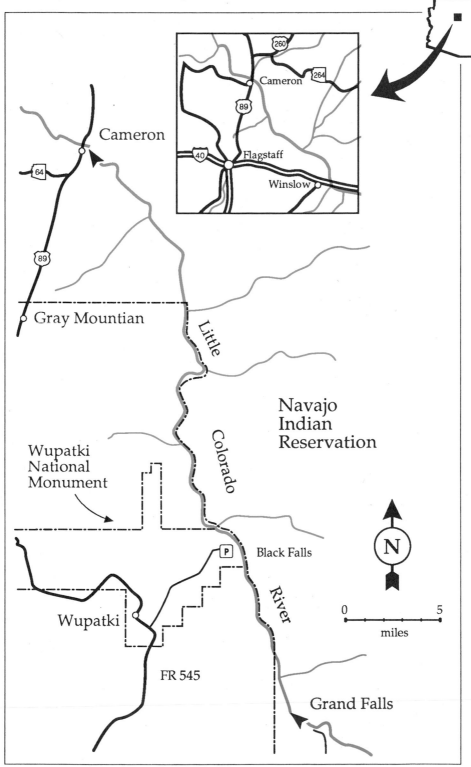

North

Cameron

Winslow

Flagstaff

Cameron

Gray Mountian

Little

Colorado

Navajo
Indian
Reservation

Wupatki
National
Monument

P Black Falls

River

Wupatki

FR 545

Grand Falls

N

0   5
miles

LITTLE COLORADO RIVER
— Cameron to Grand Canyon

LENGTH: **50 miles** SEASON: **Perennial flow**
ACCESS: **Paved road, hiking trail** ELEVATION: **4140' - 2700'**
FEATURES: **Spectacular canyon, very blue water, challenging hike**
CAUTIONS: **Indian reservation, permits required, precarious trail**
MAPS: **USGS** - Cameron North, Coconino Point, Hellhole Bend, Blue
     Springs, Salt Trail Canyon, Cape Solitude
     USBIA/USNPS- Navajo Nation, Grand Canyon National Park

A few miles below Cameron the river begins its steep descent into the Grand Canyon. A hike here is a challenging undertaking. All of the trails require strenuous climbs and some are known for their dizzying exposures. Walking down the canyon bottom when there is water in it can be difficult, even hazardous, because of the quicksand that's common there.

This remote, narrow gorge is sacred to all native peoples in the region. Blue Springs serves as a source of perennial water for the river's lower reaches. The flow from these springs is heavily laden with calcium which gives the water its azure color and accounts for the bizarre travertine deposits that line the streambanks. At river's end, where the blue waters stain the flow of the much larger Colorado, the Grand Canyon officially begins.

ACCESS: Drive US 89 north from Flagstaff to Cameron, where the road crosses the river. Just south of Cameron AZ 64 leads west to Grand Canyon National Park. Blue Springs Trail leads down a drainage off the road to Cape Solitude from Desert View. Or follow the Tanner Trail to the Beamer Trail to the River.

FACILITIES: There is a developed campground in GCNP at Desert View. Other facilities both in the park and at Cameron.

WILDLIFE: Canyon wrens trill among the cliffs and ravens croak overhead. At the Colorado conflu-ence a few humpback chubs still survive. An endangered species now, these fish crowded all Grand Canyon waters before Glen Canyon Dam.

CAUTIONS: The Navajo Tribe requires permits for all activities. GCNP requires one for backpacking. Demand is high, so apply in advance. This area is sacred to native peoples. Be respectful; don't disturb cultural sites. The river is too dangerous to boat and the Navajos don't allow it anyway.

INFORMATION: Navajo Nation; Grand Canyon National Park

USES:

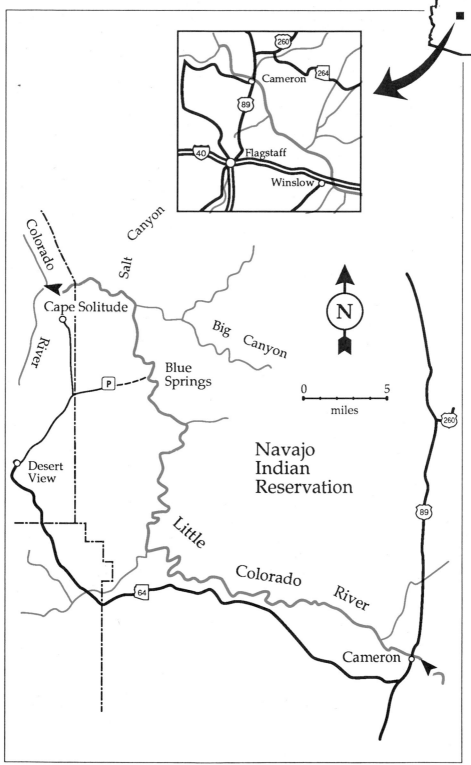

PARIA RIVER — US 89 to Lees Ferry

LENGTH: **41 miles**
ACCESS: **Paved road**
FEATURES: **Narrow, scenic canyon; wilderness setting**
CAUTIONS: **Flash floods, long hike**
MAPS: **USGS -** West Clark Bench; Bridger Point, UT. Wrather Arch, Water
  Pockets, Ferry Swale; Lees Ferry, AZ.
  USBLM - Paria Canyon Wilderness

SEASON: **Perennial flow**
ELEVATION: **4320' - 3151'**

S tarting in Utah's Bryce Canyon National Park, the Paria River flows through an extremely narrow, deep gorge as it makes its last plunge to the Colorado River. This is one of the few slot canyons that was not lost when Lake Powell inundated Glen Canyon and its tributaries. The hike through it is rewarding and challenging. The trail follows the sandy and cobbly streambed.

In addition to the spectacular scenery offered by the sheer canyon walls, one should also be on the lookout for pictographs (please leave them undisturbed for the next visitor). Twenty-two miles from the upper trailhead, Wrather Canyon enters from the south. At its upper end, 200 foot Wrather Arch is possibly the most outstanding geological feature along the Paria.

ACCESS: <u>Upper end</u>: Take US 89 west from Page about 30 miles to the White House turnoff and the trailhead. <u>Lower end</u>: Take US 89 111 miles north from Flagstaff, then US 89A for 14 miles, to the Lees Ferry turnoff.

FACILITIES: There is a National Park Service developed campground at Lees Ferry and a primitive one at the trailhead. Commercial facilities are available at Page and along both US 89 and 89A.

WILDLIFE: Desert bighorn sheep have been reintroduced here, but they frequently fall prey to the area's

mountain lions. The stream is home to a number of threatened and endangered fish including the woundfin minnow.

CAUTIONS: Overnight hiking permits are required from the Arizona Strip Interpretive Assoc. Paria Canyon and Buckskin Gulch are extremely narrow; a flash flood here could be fatal. Check the weather report and camp on high ground. Fees required.

INFORMATION: Bureau of Land Management, Arizona Strip Interpretive Association.

USES:

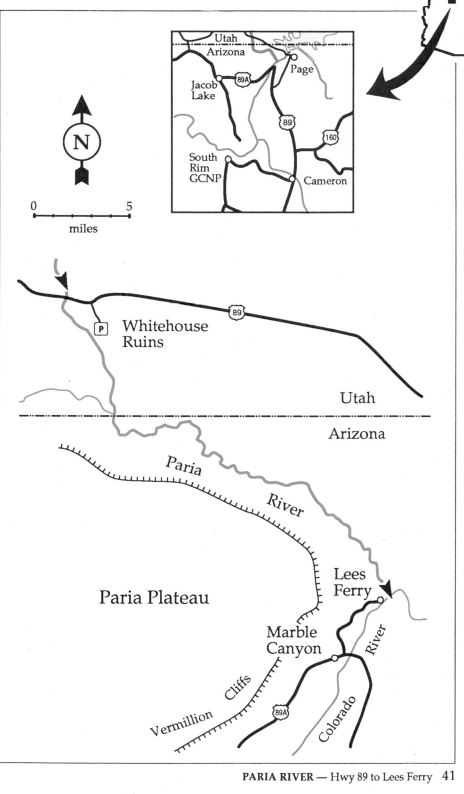

VIRGIN RIVER — Virgin River Gorge

LENGTH: **20 miles** SEASON: **Late March**
ACCESS: **Paved road, dirt road (HCV)** ELEVATION: **2690' - 1846'**
FEATURES: **Scenic canyon, easy access, boatable stream**
CAUTIONS: **Short, unpredictable season, cross-stream fences**
MAPS: **USGS -** Purgatory Canyon, Mountain Sheep Spring, Littlefield
       USBLM - Arizona Strip District

T he Virgin River flows through a scenic desert gorge populated by rare animals that have adapted to life in this harsh environment. Most of the time it is a shallow, braided stream twisting over a broad bed of gravel and sand. Occasionally it becomes a muddy flood swollen by upstream thunderstorms. About three years out of four it has a two or three week boating season during the spring run-off.

Interstate 15 offers convenient access to what was once an all but inaccessible area. People regularly stop to photograph the scenery, play in the stream, or hike in the gorge. The stream offers some sandy beaches, cool wading pools, and occasional shade. The surrounding area provides challenging hikes through a unique environment.

ACCESS: I-15 parallels the stream through most of the Virgin River Gorge. Popular put-ins are at the Cedar Pockets Recreation Site, 21 miles south of St. George, at the mouth of the gorge, and at Man-O War Bridge, St. George, UT. Lower access: At the Littlefield Ranch Exit, take the frontage road east 1.5 miles to a road to the river (private property).

FACILITIES: There is a developed USBLM campground at the Cedar Pockets Exit, 21 miles south of St. George, UT.

WILDLIFE: Desert bighorn sheep are occasionally seen along the river. Threatened desert tortoises inhabit desert areas near Littlefield. The river is home to three of the rarest fish in the world-Virgin River roundtail chub, Virgin River spinedace and woundfin minnow. Mexican black hawks nest here and possibly peregrine falcon also.

CAUTIONS: Although people use the I-15 bridge as a put-in, it is illegal to stop along it. Watch for cross-stream fences when boating. Downriver access is on private property. The highway is bordered by wilderness areas on both sides: motorized access is prohibited.

INFORMATION: U.S. Bureau of Land Management, Arizona Strip District.

USES:

class III possible   fee

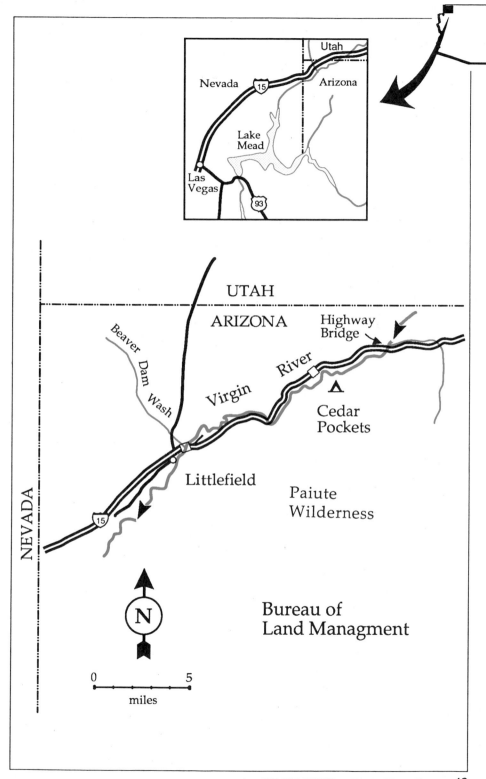

North

Utah

Nevada
15

Arizona

Lake
Mead

Las
Vegas

93

UTAH

ARIZONA

Highway
Bridge

Beaver Dam Wash

Virgin   River

Cedar
Pockets

NEVADA

Littlefield

Paiute
Wilderness

15

N

Bureau of
Land Managment

0   5
miles

Arizona Rivers and Streams Guide

Western Section

Bill Williams River
Burro Creek
Colorado River
Santa Maria River

BILL WILLIAMS RIVER

LENGTH: **34 miles**   SEASON: **Perennial flow**
ACCESS: **Paved road/dirt road (HCV)**   ELEVATION: **1050' - 450'**
FEATURES: **Scenic canyon, desert marsh, wildlife refuge**
CAUTIONS: **Summer heat, remote area, difficult access**
MAPS: **USGS -** Mount Hope, Scratch Canyon, Burro Mesa, Bozarth Mesa,
        Negro Ed, Grayback Mountains, Kaiser Spring, Greenwood Peak
        USBLM - Kingman Planning Area

The Bill Williams River flows through two distinct area. Just below
Alamo Dam it enters a narrow canyon where close-set walls limit the
only means of access to walking down the streambed. Usually, that's
no problem since flows from the dam are routinely low. A few daredevils
have boated this stretch during its infrequent high flows, but those who
know the river say the best way to see its scenic canyon is to hike it.

Six or seven miles below the dam the canyon opens up and the riverbed
spreads across a broad plain dotted with cottonwoods. Near the Colorado
River it enters an extensive marsh that provides an extremely productive
wetland habitat here in the midst of the nation's hottest desert. Birdwatching
is popular in this backwater of the Bill Williams River National Wildlife
Refuge, where a number of rare species may be seen.

ACCESS: <u>From Wickenburg:</u> Go
west on US 60 to Wenden, then north
on the Alamo Lake Road. Or continue past Wenden to Hope, north on
AZ 72 to Parker, then north to
Buckskin Mountain State Park.

FACILITIES: There are developed
State Park campgrounds at Alamo
Lake and at Buckskin Mountain
State Park. Other facilities are
available at Wickenburg and Parker.

WILDLIFE: The canyon below
Alamo Dam is pristine riparian
habitat. Look for water-loving birds
like green kingfishers and endangered southern bald eagles (which

nest here). There are beavers and
one hiker reported seeing a mountain lion. In the marsh there is a
good chance of seeing endangered
Yuma clapper rails, threatened black
rails and several species of waterfowl.

CAUTIONS: Boating this canyon
when the water is high enough to do
so is dangerous. Stay off it unless
you are an expert. The canyon itself
is a remote area. Seasonal closure to
recreational activities Jan. 1-June 1.

INFORMATION: USBLM, Lake
Havasu Field Office; Arizona State
Parks

USES:

fee

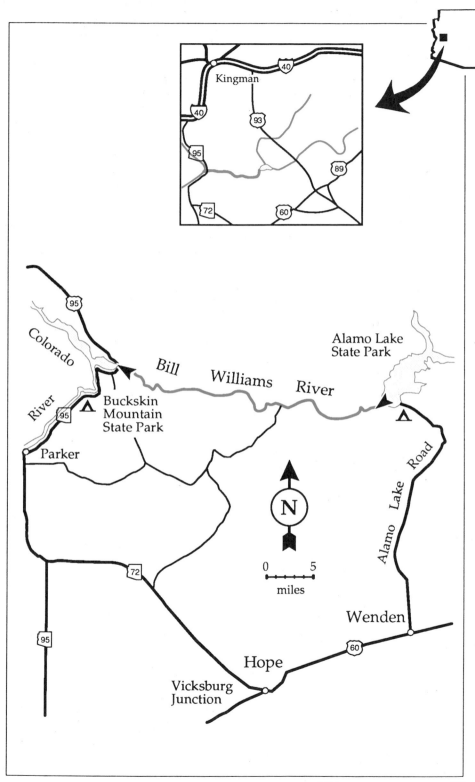

BURRO CREEK — Florence Creek to US 93 Bridge

LENGTH: **28 miles**
ACCESS: **Paved road, hiking trail**
FEATURES: **Spectacular canyon, raptor habitat, secluded pools**
CAUTIONS: **Summer heat, remote area, flash floods, restricted access**
SEASON: **Perennial flow**
ELEVATION: **3100' - 1800'**
MAPS: **USGS** - Mount Hope, Scratch Canyon, Burro Mesa, Bozarth Mesa, Negro Ed, Grayback Mountains, Kaiser Spring, Greenwood Peak
USBLM - Kingman District

Burro Creek makes a dramatic first impression as its deep canyon passes under US 93. Those willing to boulder-hop upstream will find that spectacular scenery is only one of the features this area offers. Home to what may be the most diverse community of raptors in North America, it is one of the few places where wintering northern bald eagles and threatened southern bald eagles meet. The largest concentration of nesting Mexican black hawks on the continent can be found here.

Upstream, canyon walls drop back to make room for cottonwoods and willows. Animal species increase. You can also enjoy one of the many pools that persist even when the stream seems to have stopped flowing.

ACCESS: From Phoenix, drive northwest along AZ/US 93 to the river. South of the bridge is a USBLM campground and the trailhead. Access to upper Burro Creek is through the mining area of the Cyprus Bagdad Company. Contact the company in advance to secure a permit and arrange for a guide to take you across company property.

FACILITIES: USBLM campground and waterplay area south of the US 93 Bridge. Good area for picnicking, photography and history/archaeology.

WILDLIFE: This area supports an incredibly diversity of wildlife including threatened Mexican black hawks, zone-tailed hawks, northern and southern bald eagles, golden eagles and peregrine falcons; numerous reptiles such as western diamondback and speckled rattlesnakes, gila monsters and zebra-tailed lizards; and mammals like mule deer, javelina and beaver.

CAUTIONS: This narrow canyon is prone to flash floods even when the sky above the canyon in completely clear. The boulders are very slippery. Burro Canyon is very isolated. Small problems can easily become big ones this far from help.

INFORMATION: Kingman Field Office; Cyprus Bagdad Company; Wickenburg Chamber of Commerce

USES:

fee

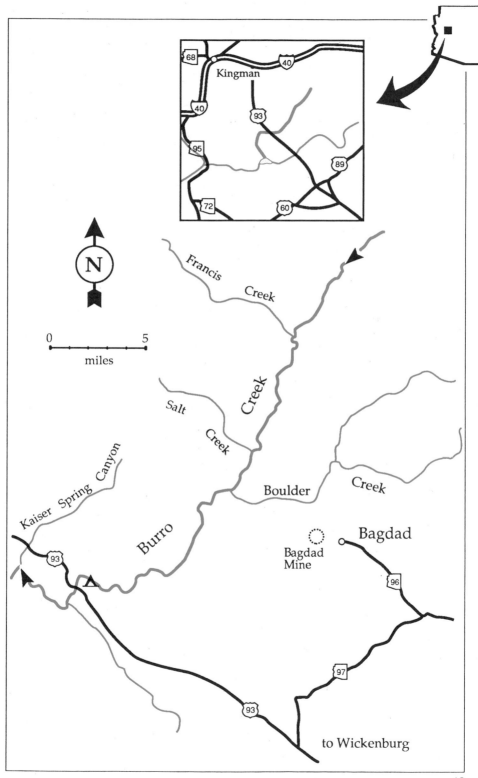

COLORADO RIVER — Black Canyon

LENGTH: **13 miles**   SEASON: **All year**
ACCESS: **Paved road**   ELEVATION: **720' - 680'**
FEATURES: **Scenic canyon, hot springs, guided trips, desert bighorns**
CAUTIONS: **Steep, rocky shoreline; powerboats; health hazard**
MAPS: **USGS -** Hoover Dam, Ringbolt Rapids, Willow Beach
　　　USNPS - Lake Mead National Recreation Area

T his is a popular stretch of river for both power boaters and canoers. One of its biggest attractions is the scenery. Actually, this was considered part of the Grand Canyon, at least by river runners, until Lake Mead buried the river. When the waters of downstream Lake Mohave are low, Ringbolt Rapids, historically the final obstacle of the Grand Canyon run, surfaces as a riffle along this stretch.

　　The hot springs in nearby side canyons are a powerful attraction here too. However, they contain an amoeba (Naegleria fowleri) common to hot springs that can cause sickness and even death. This parasite infects humans through their nasal passages. It has caused one known fatality (1987).

ACCESS: <u>Hoover Dam</u>: Follow US 93 north from Kingman 71 miles to Hoover Dam. LMNRA provides access for small boats at the bottom of the dam. <u>Willow Beach</u>: Turn west off US 93, 14 miles south of Hoover Dam to Willow Beach Landing.

FACILITIES: RV hook-ups, a motel, restaurant, store and raft trips are available at Willow Beach. There is a canoe livery and car shuttle service in Boulder City, Nevada. Other facilities are located in Boulder City and Kingman.

WILDLIFE: This is an excellent place to see lots of desert bighorn sheep, a rare species that has been re-established. The best time is late summer. The river is stocked with trout.

CAUTIONS: LMNRA has a pamphlet outlining precautions you can take to avoid infection by the hot springs amoeba. Power boats are a hazard to canoers.

INFORMATION: Lake Mead National Recreation Area; US Bureau of Reclamation

USES:

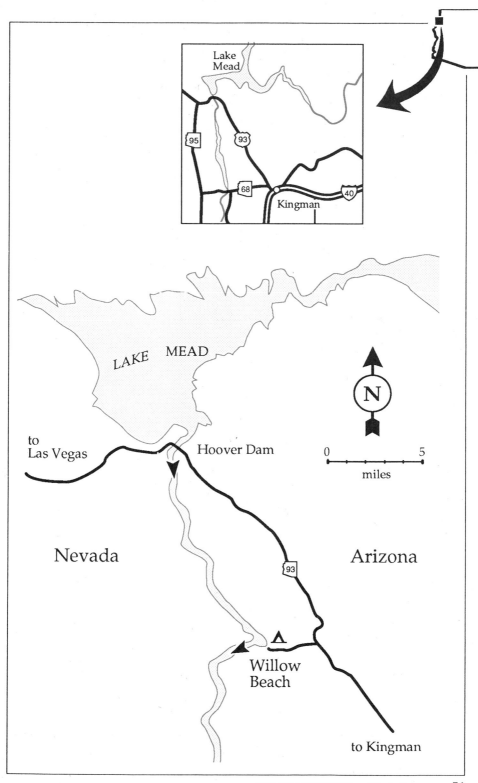

COLORADO RIVER — Davis Dam to Lake Havasu

LENGTH: **54 miles**   SEASON: **All year**
ACCESS: **Paved road/dirt road**   ELEVATION: **520' - 475'**
FEATURES: **Wildlife refuge, wetland, largemouth bass fishing**
CAUTIONS: **Fire and camping prohibited within refuge**
MAPS: **USGS -** (1:100,000) Davis Dam, Needles
      USFWS - Havasu National Wildlife Refuge

This area offers a number of diverse recreational opportunities, including everything from waterskiing and jet boating to backcountry (well, almost) canoeing. It's an excellent area for fishing and birdwatching, both in the marsh and along the river, and there are a number of convenient campgrounds right at the edge of the water.

Canoeing the stretch through Topock Gorge and the Havasu National Wildlife Refuge is gaining in popularity and has attracted national media attention. Power boats are permitted in the refuge, but all waters outside the main navigational channel are "no-wake" zones.

ACCESS: <u>Davis Dam</u>: take AZ 68 west from US 93 just north of Kingman. Topock on the Arizona side and Park Moabi on the California side are located just north of I-40. A convenient take-out is located at Castle Rock off AZ 95, about 15 miles south of I-40.

FACILITIES: Developed campgrounds, picnic areas, and other facilities are available at a number of sites along the river. Canoes and other boats may be rented at Lake Havasu City.

WILDLIFE: The marshes along the river here teem with ducks, geese, and other species of water-loving birds. Some of the latter include white-faced ibises, great blue herons, and the endangered Yuma clapper rail.

CAUTIONS: Water skiing, fires, and camping are prohibited within the national wildlife refuge.

INFORMATION: US Fish and Wildlife Service; US Bureau of Reclamation

USES:

warm   fees

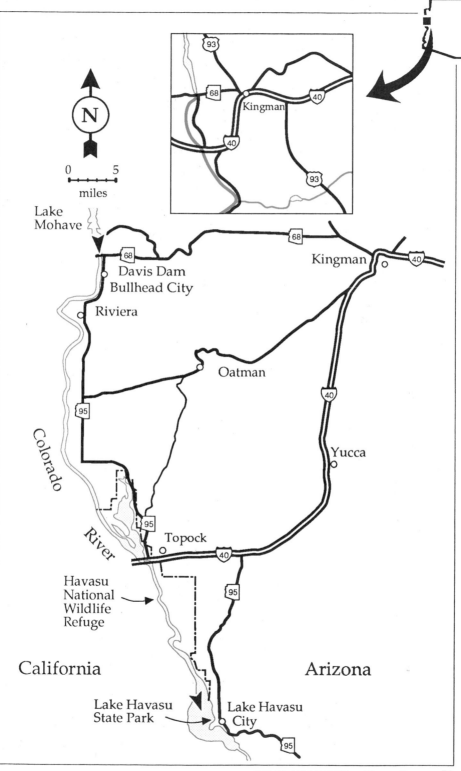

Lake
Mohave

68

Davis Dam
Bullhead City

Riviera

Kingman

40

68

95

Colorado

Oatman

40

Yucca

River

95

Topock

40

Havasu
National
Wildlife
Refuge

95

California

Arizona

Lake Havasu
State Park

Lake Havasu
City

95

0   5
miles

N

93

68

Kingman

40

40

93

COLORADO RIVER — Parker Dam to Ehrenberg

LENGTH: **70 miles**
ACCESS: **Paved road**
FEATURES: **Scenic canyon, easy access, waterskiing**
CAUTIONS: **Speedboats and personal water craft are dominant summer river users.**
MAPS: **USGS** - (1:100,000) Parker, Blythe

SEASON: **All year**
ELEVATION: **400' - 380'**

This is a scenic stretch of river which passes through several beautiful geographic areas, including high red rock cliffs, sand dunes, reeded riparian areas and monolithic mountain cliffs. The current moves along at a good rate and the river has all that's necessary for a day trip or a longer vacation.

Sun-seeking retirees flock to the river during winter months for the better than average fishing, many who live in the many full-service RV resorts and campgrounds along the riverfront. The summer months see younger vacationers on the river, who enjoy speed boating, personal watercraft, water-skiing, tubing and nighttime fishing.

However, pontoon boats for fishing or just cruising are a popular mode of transportation all through the year. All water enthusiasts are welcome at any time and boat cooperatively so that everyone enjoys this beautiful and unique stretch of the Colorado.

ACCESS: Take the Lake Havasu Exit from I-40 and drive south 35 miles on AZ 95, or drive north on AZ 95 from the Quartzite exit on I-10. Ehrenberg is located on I-95 at the California state line.

FACILITIES: There are a number of campgrounds, boat ramps and picnic areas along both sides of the river, including those at Buckskin Mtn. State Park. Other facilities are available along AZ 95 and in Parker and Lake Havasu City.

WILDLIFE: Bighorn sheep and waterfowl may be seen here during the off-season after the crowds have gone. Largemouth and striped bass inhabit the river.

CAUTIONS: Small boaters and canoeists may wish to visit the Parker area during the winter or fall seasons when the river traffic is lighter.

INFORMATION: Parker Chamber of Commerce (www.coloradoriverinfo.com/parker); Buckskin Mtn. State Park; USBLM Lake Havasu & Yuma Field Offices

USES:

warm

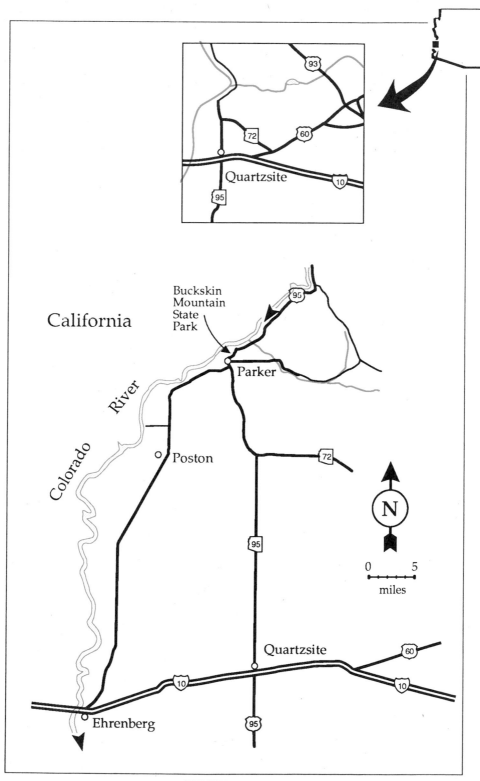

COLORADO RIVER — Ehrenberg to Imperial Dam

LENGTH: **66 miles**   SEASON: **All year**
ACCESS: **Paved road/dirt road**   ELEVATION: **380' - 200'**
FEATURES: **Wildlife refuges, large riparian area, canoe rentals**
CAUTIONS: **Limited access, camping restrictions, crowded channel**
MAPS: **USGS -** (1:100,000) Parker, Blythe, Trigo, Yuma
          USF&WS - Cibola, Imperial National Wildlife Refuges

Two national wildlife refuges along this stretch make it of high interest to small boaters. Within their boundaries the river occupies two separate channels. One is man-made. Its straight, deep course provides a popular environment for powerboaters. The other follows the historic river bed. In its quiet backwaters an observant paddler can see Canada geese and other waterfowl by the score, perhaps even catching a glimpse of the endangered Yuma clapper rail. Along both sides of the river a few old mining sites provide popular stopping places.

Those who keep a sharp eye out might spy a Yuma puma, perhaps the rarest subspecies of mountain lion in existence. These cats are believed to still prowl the tangled bosques that border the lower Colorado River. They have recently been designated a threatened species in Arizona. The last one was seen in 1972.

ACCESS: Headgate Dam: Drive northwest out of Parker on AZ spur 95. Access to the more popular lower portion of this stretch is available at Ehrenberg on I-95, off CA 78 at Palo Verde, CA, and at Martinez Lake, AZ, 11 miles off AZ 95.

FACILITIES: Campgrounds, restaurants, lodging, and other facilities are available in Parker, Quartzite and Lake Martinez, Arizona as well as Blythe and Palo Verde, California. There are canoe and pontoon boat rentals in Lake Martinez.

WILDLIFE: Tens of thousands of waterfowl crowd the backwaters of the refuges during the spring and fall migrations. The stream supports a warm water fishery including striped bass.

CAUTIONS: In the wildlife refuges camping is prohibited, and water skiing is permitted only in the main navigational channel.

INFORMATION: Cibola National Wildlife Refuge; Imperial National Wildlife Refuge; Parker Chamber of Commerce

USES:
warm   fee

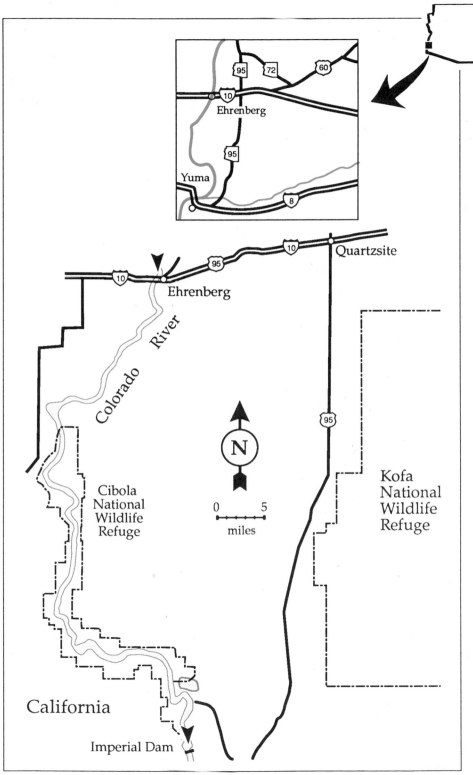

West

COLORADO RIVER — Laguna Dam to Morelos Dam

LENGTH: 21 miles
ACCESS: Paved road
SEASON: All year
ELEVATION: 156' - 100'
FEATURES: Sea and shore birds, convenient access, canoe rentals
CAUTIONS: Sunburn, private land
MAPS: USGS - (1:100,000) Yuma
      USBLM Yuma District

H ere the mighty Colorado that has brawled its way through the Grand Canyon twists slowly among broad sand bars and tall cottonwoods before disappearing completely into the diversion ditches at Morelos Dam. This placid last hurrah is a far cry from the river's tumultous birth high in the Rockies, but for a small-boater it can still provide a rewarding day out on the water. The Sea of Cortez is near enough that sea birds and shore birds are common visitors here, combining with riparian species to provide a unique experience for birdwatchers. Look for willets, curlews, and turnstones along with several species of gulls. Fishing is good too, with striped bass, catfish, and largemouth bass attracting the greatest interest.

Access is easy here as the river runs right through the city of Yuma. Residents consider this stretch something of a local secret, but are quite willing to share that secret with newcomers. In August, the city of Yuma celebrates its relationship with the river by hosting a raft race.

ACCESS: Drive north out of Yuma on Laguna Dam Road to the river at the base of the dam. The river is accessible under the 4th street bridge. On the California side use the Winterhaven Exit and drive south to levee road. The river is accessible at a number of points off this road.

FACILITIES: There is a developed campground at Laguna Dam and a number of primitive sites at other access points. All other facilities are available in Yuma.

WILDLIFE: Seabirds and shore-birds combine with riparian species to provide excellent birdwatching. The river supports a warmwater fishery of striped bass, largemouth bass and flathead catfish.

CAUTIONS: There are some power boats to watch out for, and private property borders the river.

INFORMATION: Yuma Chamber of Commerce; US Bureau of Land Management, Yuma District

USES:

warm

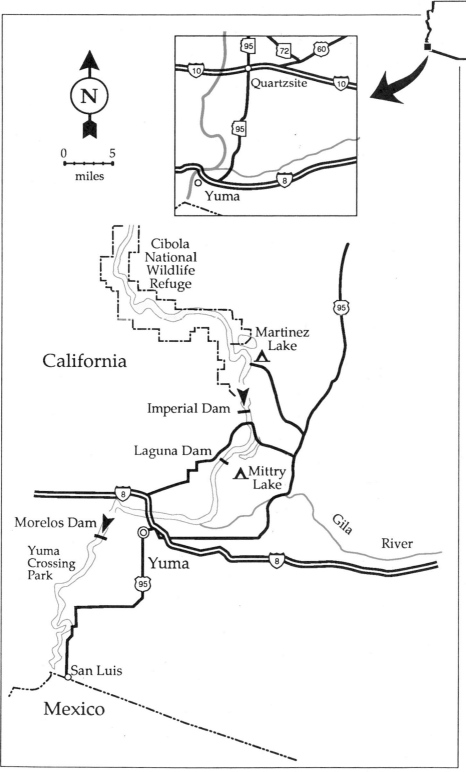

SANTA MARIA

LENGTH: **27 miles** SEASON: **Intermittent flow**
ACCESS: **Paved road/dirt road (HCV)** ELEVATION: **1800' - 1200'**
FEATURES: **Unique vegetation, scenic desert, watchable wildlife**
CAUTIONS: **Intermittent flows, summer heat, private property**
MAPS: **USGS -** Ives Peak, Arrastra Mtn SE, Palmerita Ranch
　　　　USBLM - Kingman District

T his may be a humble stream, but it certainly does keep interesting company. Where the river crosses US 93, the Mojave and Sonoran Deserts mingle and Joshua trees and saguaro cactuses stand side by side. This diverse habitat supports watchable wildlife that includes everything from mountain lions to belted kingfishers.

Where the river joins the Big Sandy River above Alamo Lake, you may see endangered southern bald eagles along with white pelicans, Franklin's gulls, and snowy egrets. On years when the eagles nest successfully, the US Fish & Wildlife Service sets up a visitor information center where you can learn more about these rare birds.

ACCESS: From Phoenix drive northwest on AZ/US 93 (the Wickenburg Highway) to the river. North of the bridge, a gated, unmaintained road offers access to a few primitive campsites and the riverbed. Or turn west off AZ 93 on a dirt road 22 miles north of Wickenburg. Follow this road through the little community of Wayside to a fork four miles beyond and take the right fork to Brown's Crossing and the Eagle Watch center.

FACILITIES: There is a developed State Parks campground at Alamo Lake and a USFWS bald eagle information center at the upper end of the lake. Good area for horseback riding and photography.

WILDLIFE: Gambel's quail, cactus wren, and white wing doves are common all along the river. The nearby mountains hold good populations of mountain lions. A pair of endangered southern bald eagles nests along the river near Alamo Lake. There you can see white pelicans, snowy egrets and black shouldered kites, too.

CAUTIONS: Entering state trust land in the area requires written permit. Respect private property and mining claim boundaries. Avoid disturbing nesting eagles.

INFORMATION: Kingman Field Office; AZ State Lands Dept.; Wickenburg Chamber of Commerce

USES:

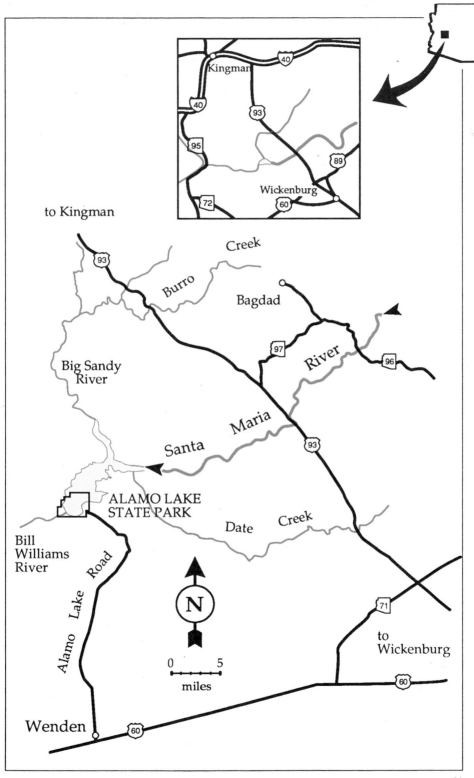

to Kingman

Kingman

Wickenburg

Creek

Burro

Bagdad

Big Sandy
River

River

Santa

Maria

ALAMO LAKE
STATE PARK

Date

Creek

Bill
Williams
River

Alamo Lake Road

N

0 5
miles

to
Wickenburg

Wenden

Arizona Rivers and Streams Guide

Southern Section

Aravaipa Creek
Cave Creek
Cienega Creek
Gardner Canyon
Hot Springs Canyon
Madera Canyon
Redfield Canyoin
Sabino Creek
San Pedro River
Sonoita Creek
Sycamore Creek

Aravaipa Creek, Tanna Thornburg

ARAVAIPA CREEK

LENGTH: **34 miles** SEASON: **Perennial flow**
ACCESS: **Dirt rd (HCV), hiking trail** ELEVATION: **3065' - 2150'**
FEATURES: **Scenic canyon, riparian wilderness, colorful birds**
CAUTIONS: **Summer heat, permit required, no pets**
MAPS: **USGS** - Klondyke, Booger Canyon, Brandenburg Mtn.
  USBLM - Safford District

A ravaipa Creek offers an experience that is quite rare in Arizona (or anywhere in the Southwest for that matter) — a wilderness stroll along a bubbling stream shaded by lush greenery. The forest of tall cottonwoods, sycamores and ash that the creek supports is alive with birds. Its waters remain at a healthy level year-round, providing critical habitat for a number of native fish species. From the Canyon bottom impressive views of the high cliffs and peaks of the Galiuro Mountains contrast with intimate views of streamside wildflowers. The smell of fresh water and lush vegetation mixed with dry desert air is unforgettable.

Walking at a leisurely pace all the way through Aravaipa Canyon takes about ten to fifteen hours, if you pass up all the tempting side canyons. Most people enter and leave by the same access point due to the difficulty of arranging a car shuttle. Many spend a night or two. Writer Edward Abbey made famous an encounter here with a curious mountain lion. Perhaps your visit will be as memorable.

ACCESS: Turn east off AZ 77 about 20 miles north of Oracle. The trail head is at the end of this rough and rugged road (12 miles). Or leave I-10 at the Safford exit, drive 14 miles to AZ 266, then 18 miles to Bonita and another 35 miles to the trail head.

FACILITIES: There is a developed campground near the eastern access. Limited facilities are available in nearby towns.

WILDLIFE: The Aravaipa area is known for the many bird species

that can be found here, especially the Mexican black hawk. Desert bighorn are seen during cooler seasons and an occasional mountain lion may be sighted. Ringtail cats raid food supplies at night.

CAUTIONS: Required permits are limited, so apply early. Wear wading shoes. No pets are permitted.

INFORMATION: USBLM, Safford District Office

USES:

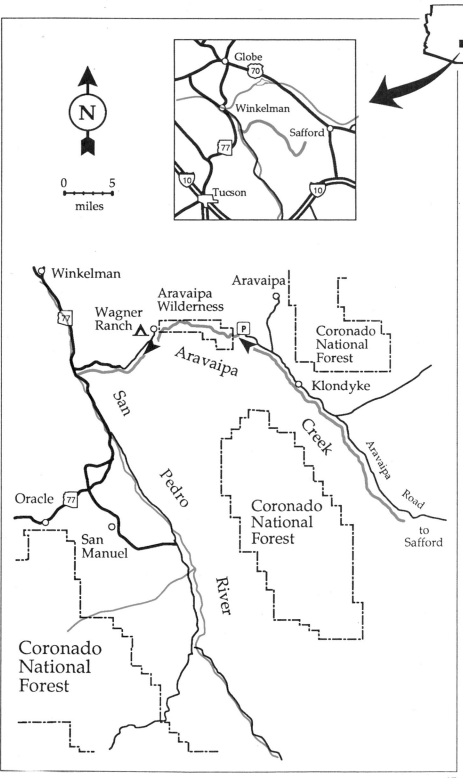

Globe
70
Winkelman
Safford
77
10
Tucson
10

N

0   5
miles

Winkelman
77
Wagner
Ranch
Aravaipa
Wilderness
Aravaipa
Aravaipa
P
Coronado
National
Forest
Klondyke
San
Creek
Pedro
Aravaipa Road
Oracle
77
San
Manuel
Coronado
National
Forest
to
Safford
River
Coronado
National
Forest

CAVE CREEK — Chiricahuas

LENGTH: **9 miles**
ACCESS: **Paved road/dirt road**
SEASON: **Perennial flow**
ELEVATION: **7000' - 5000'**
FEATURES: **Unique vegetation, scenic stream, watchable wildlife**
CAUTIONS: **Streambed route, one way access, flash floods**
MAPS: **USGS -** Chiricahua Peak, Portal Peak, Portal, Portal NE
       USFS - Coronado National Forest, Chiricahua Mountains

T his little mountain creek starts high among forests of Arizona cypress and Apache pine. It then drops into chaparral woodlands of oak and juniper. Ghost-white sycamores and gnarly cottonwoods crowd the stream bottom, providing shelter for the colorful birds who live here and shade for the birdwatchers who come to stalk them.

Cave Creek is extremely popular for family camping, hiking, and wildlife watching. Several campgrounds are located along easily accessible stretches of the stream and a number of hiking trails lead to more remote areas-including a Wilderness Area. Many people come here to find birds that they would otherwise have to travel to Mexico to see. Among those are the elegant trogon.

ACCESS: Turn south off I-10 at the Hwy 80 turnoff (just inside the New Mexico border). Follow Hwy 80 south to Portal Rd. Take that road west to Portal.

FACILITIES: A number of USFS developed campgrounds are located along both forks of the creek. There is a general store and restaurant in Portal. Southwestern Research Station, also along the creek, provides lodging on a reservation basis.

WILDLIFE: Look for elegant trogons and lots of different kinds of hummingbirds. You have a good chance of seeing a black bear or a Coues white-tailed deer. A jaguar was seen in the Chiricahuas in 1987.

CAUTIONS: Along the lower stretches of the stream, camping is permitted in developed campsites only.

INFORMATION: Coronado National Forest, Douglas Ranger District

USES:

fee

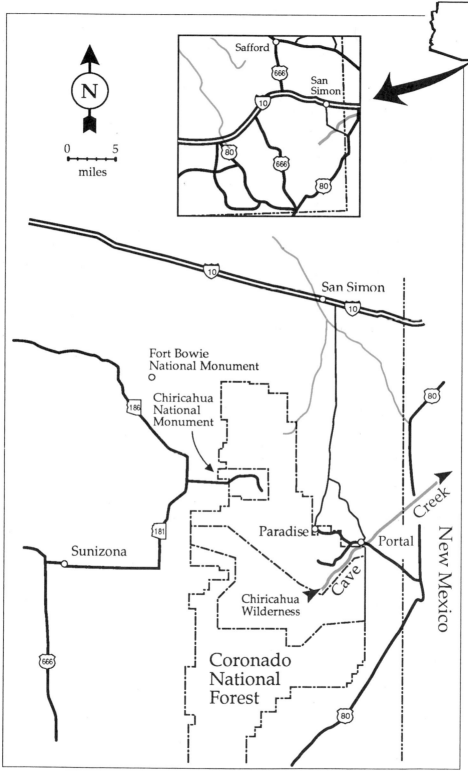

N

0   5
miles

Safford

666

San
Simon

10

80

666

80

South

10

San Simon

10

Fort Bowie
National Monument
○

Chiricahua
National
Monument

186

80

Paradise

Portal

New Mexico

Sunizona

181

Cave

Creek

Chiricahua
Wilderness

666

Coronado
National
Forest

80

CIENEGA CREEK

LENGTH: **11 miles**   SEASON: **Perennial flow**
ACCESS: **Paved road, hiking trail**   ELEVATION: **3600' - 3350'**
FEATURES: **County nature preserve, desert stream, easy access**
CAUTIONS: **Visible impacts, permit required**
MAPS: **USGS** - O'Donnell Canyon, Spring Water Canyon, The Narrows,
Rincon Peak, Vail
USBLM - Phoenix District

The lower reaches of this small desert stream are protected by Pima County as a nature preserve. The purpose is to protect the riparian habitat it supports and to provide an alternative type of flood protection to Tucson downstream. An additional benefit of that move was the preservation of the recreational opportunities it provides. The preserve offers residents of Tucson and nearby suburbs a chance to hike along the banks of a tree-lined, flowing, desert stream, to watch its wildlife, and splash in its waters.

The deeply entrenched channel flows through an area where the Sonoran and Chihuahuan deserts mix. It is bordered by a number of ancient cultural sites. The area is also popular for horseback riding.

ACCESS: Leave I-10 at the Sonoita Road Exit, 21 miles east of Tucson. Turn north on the Marsh Station Road, which parallels the river and returns to I-10 at the Pantano exit. The river is also accessible via the Vail Exit.

WILDLIFE: Low desert animals mix with riparian birds within the preserve. Killdeer, black phoebes, and great blue herons are often seen. Mule deer and javelina are common mammals. A rare fish, the longfin dace, swims in the waters

FACILITIES: Dispersed camping is available in nearby Coronado National Forest. Commercial campgrounds and other facilities are available in Tucson.

CAUTIONS: A permit is required to visit the preserve. You can get it from the Pima County Parks and Recreation Department in Tucson.

INFORMATION: Pima County Parks & Recreation Department

USES:

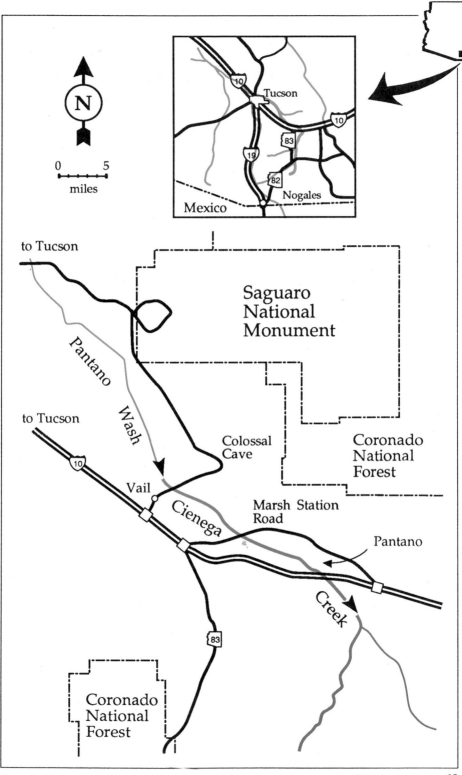

GARDNER CANYON

LENGTH: **11 miles**   SEASON: **Intermittent flow**
ACCESS: **Dirt road/hiking trail**   ELEVATION: **6500' - 4200'**
FEATURES: **Great campsites, hiking trails, caves, scenic canyon**
CAUTIONS: **High use area, caves restricted**
MAPS: **USGS** -Mt. Wrightson, Sonoita, Spring Water Canyon
      USFS - Coronado National Forest

S pacious campsites under spreading oak trees near a flowing stream provide the attraction that draws most people to Gardner Canyon. A road parallels the creek's lower reaches and provides easy access to a number of well-used streamside campsites. Upstream of Tunnel Springs, the canyon narrows and the road gets rough, finally giving way to a hiking trail that leads up the slopes of Mt. Wrightson and Josephine Peak. From here you can enjoy good views back down the canyon.

A spur off Gardner Canyon Road leads up a tributary called Cave Creek, providing access to two caves open to the public with permission. The upper stretches of both streams usually have pools deep enough to splash in.

ACCESS: About 4.5 miles north of Sonoita on AZ 83, a dirt road (FR 92) turns west to Gardner Canyon. Past Apache Springs, FR 92 turns north up Cave Creek. FR 785 continues along Gardner to the head of Trail #143, and FR 4084 leads to Cave of the Bells.

FACILITIES: Nearest facilities are in the towns of Sonoita and Patagonia.

WILDLIFE: There are a lot of hummingbirds here. Occasionally a trogon strays over from Madera Canyon. Mammals in the area include Coues whitetail deer, coatimundis and ringtailed cats.

CAUTIONS: To enter the Cave of the Bells you must get a key from the Tucson or Nogales offices of the Forest Service. For Onyx Cave contact the Escabrosa Grotto, Inc. in Tucson.

INFORMATION: Coronado National Forest, Nogales Ranger District; Escabrosa Grotto, Inc.

USES:

primitive

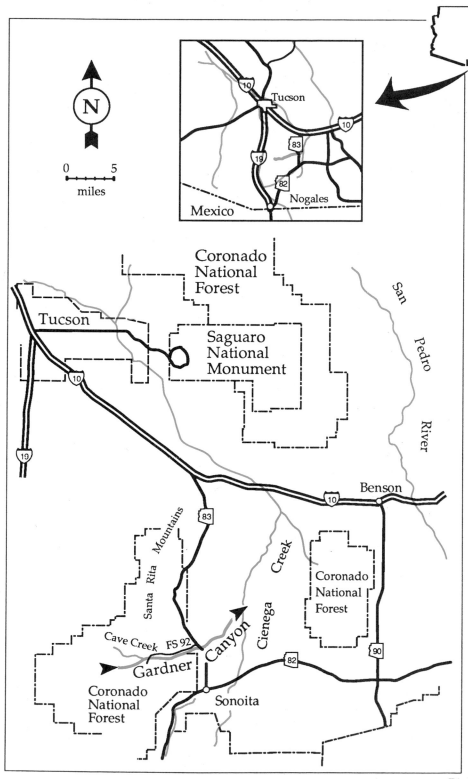

HOT SPRINGS CANYON

LENGTH: **13 miles**   SEASON: **Perennial flow**
ACCESS: **Dirt road, hiking trail**   ELEVATION: **5000' - 3200'**
FEATURES: **Scenic canyon, nature preserve, virgin stream**
CAUTIONS: **Remote area, in-stream hiking, rough roads**
MAPS: **USGS** -Hookers Hot Springs, Soza Mesa
          USFS - Coronado National Forest

H ot Springs Canyon is a smaller, more accessible version of spectacular Redfield Canyon to the north. Both are just beginning to attract the interest of hikers and nature lovers. Uniquely eroded rock formations and narrow slot-side canyons make this isolated area well worth visiting. Like Redfield, its native fish population is uncompromised. Its inner gorge supports an excellent riparian zone with perennial pools for wading and cooling off.

Hiking is the main recreational activity here, but the canyon is also a good place for wildlife watching. Part of the stream lies within the boundaries of the Muleshoe Ranch Preserve owned by The Nature Conservancy. It is advisable to call ahead before visiting.

ACCESS: From the West Willcox Exit off I-10, drive north to Cascabel Road. Turn west and drive 14 miles to Hookers Hot Springs Road. Drive to the Muleshoe Ranch Preserve on Hot Springs Canyon.

FACILITIES: Primitive camping is permitted on National Forest and BLM lands. No facilities: stock up with provisions before leaving Willcox.

WILDLIFE: The stream is home to a number of native fishes including the longfin dace, Gila and mountain suckers. A variety of interesting birds can be seen including zone-tailed hawks, gray hawks, western tanagers, and shy, yellow-billed cuckoos.

CAUTIONS: The upper access road is extremely rugged; a 4WD is advisable. This is a very isolated canyon; come prepared for a wilderness hike.

INFORMATION: Coronado National Forest, Safford Ranger District; BLM, Safford District; Nature Conservancy, Muleshoe Preserve

USES:

primitive

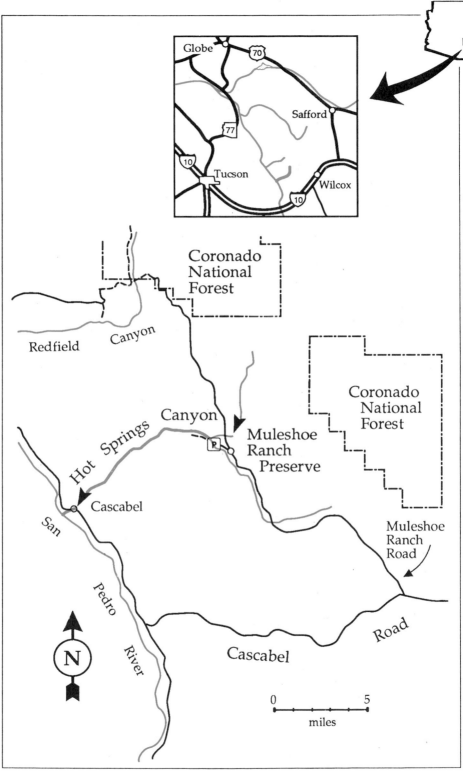

MADERA CANYON

LENGTH: **11 miles** SEASON: **Perennial flow**
ACCESS: **Dirt road, hiking trail** ELEVATION: **6500' - 2900'**
FEATURES: **Exotic birds, scenic canyon, hiking trails**
CAUTIONS: **Some private property, occasional crowds**
MAPS: **USGS -** Mt. Hopkins, Green Valley
  USFS - Coronado National Forest, Santa Rita Mtns

Madera Canyon is famous for its birds, but most famous of all for the elegant trogon. The range of that parrot-like fugitive from the tropics extends here from Mexico. Birders travel thousands of miles to add it to their life lists. Over the years so many bird watchers have come that the Santa Rita Lodge was built to provide them with shelter. A number of these nature-loving pilgrims fell so in love with the place that they built their homes here.

The creek drops out of the high reaches of the Santa Rita Mountains through a forest that changes from ponderosa and mixed conifer to scrub oak woodlands. Cottonwoods, willows, and mesquites line its banks, providing the rich habitat that supports such a diverse community.

ACCESS: About 23 miles south of Tucson at Green Valley, exit I-19 and drive east through Continental to FR 62. Follow this road about 7 miles to FR 70. Turn south on FR 70 to the canyon.

FACILITIES: There is a USFS developed campground at Bog Springs along the creek and two picnic areas nearby. The lodge offers rooms, a gift shop and information. Other facilities are available in Tucson.

WILDLIFE: The trogon is the star here, but the area is also well known for its large population of humming-birds. Mountain lions, black bears, mule deer and javelina have been seen in the canyon.

CAUTIONS: Respect the privacy of residents, both human and other-wise. Mountain lions have shown a taste for pets here recently. Hiking trails up Mt. Wrightson are steep and strenuous.

INFORMATION: Coronado National Forest, Nogales Ranger District

USES:

fee trogons

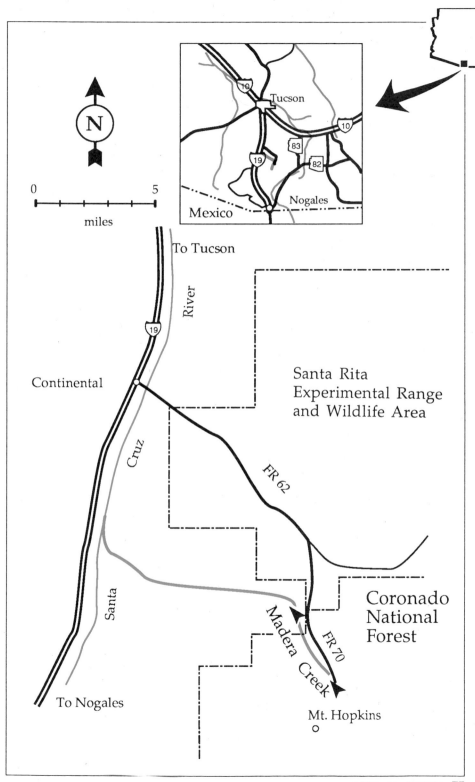

N

0   5
miles

Tucson

Mexico   Nogales

To Tucson

River

Continental

Santa Rita
Experimental Range
and Wildlife Area

Cruz

FR 62

Santa

Coronado
National
Forest

Madera Creek

FR 70

To Nogales

Mt. Hopkins

South

REDFIELD CANYON

LENGTH: **14 miles**   SEASON: **Perennial flow**
ACCESS: **Dirt road, hiking trail**   ELEVATION: **5000' - 3000'**
FEATURES: **Spectacular canyon, wilderness setting, virgin stream**
CAUTIONS: **Difficult access (4WD), remote area, in-stream hiking**
MAPS: **USGS** -Bassett Peak, Cherry Spring Peak, Redington
       USFS - Coronado National Forest

This is a very rugged canyon that is extremely difficult to get to, but that's one of the main reasons to go. The spectacular scenery is another. Because of its extreme isolation this creek is one of the last in the state to support a totally native fishery. The canyon it has formed is deep and steep. The uniquely eroded formations along its walls will make you reach for your camera again and again. This place deserves to be enjoyed with care.

      The road to the canyon's upper stretches is long and rugged. It requires a four wheel drive. The road to its lower end leaves you at the top of a steep, hot climb to the canyon bottom. Once you get there you'll find it well worth the effort, with secluded pools and lots of shade.

ACCESS: From West Willcox Exit off I-10 drive north on Fort Grant Road to Cascabel Road. Turn west and drive 14 miles to Hookers Hot Springs Road. Drive to the Muleshoe Ranch Preserve and continue on to Jackson Canyon and the trailhead. Markham Canyon Road out of Redington leads to a trail into Redfield.

FACILITIES: Primitive camping is permitted on National Forest and BLM lands. Stock up with provisions before you leave Willcox and Tucson.

WILDLIFE: The stream is home to a number of native fish, including the longfin and speckled dace, Gila and mountain suckers. Birds that can be seen include zone-tailed hawks and yellow-billed cuckoos. There are desert bighorn sheep too.

CAUTIONS: The upper access road is extremely rugged beyond Muleshoe. A 4WD is advisable. This is a very isolated canyon; come prepared for a wilderness hike.

INFORMATION: Coronado National Forest, Safford Ranger District; BLM, Safford District; Nature Conservancy, Muleshoe Preserve.

USES:

primitive

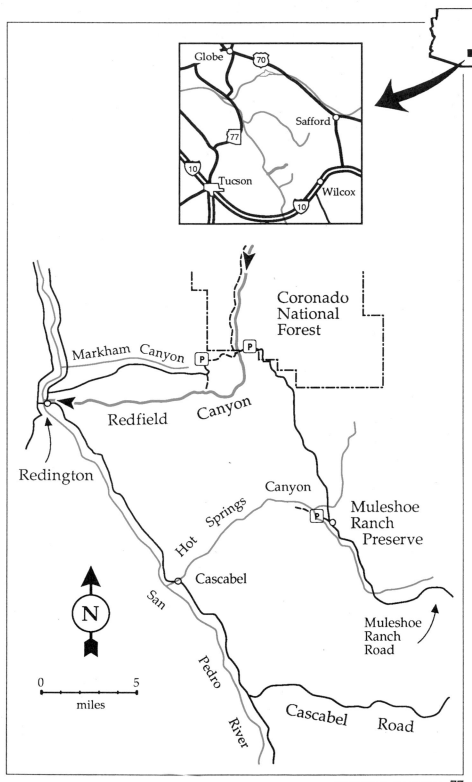

SABINO CREEK

LENGTH: **12 miles** SEASON: **Perennial flow**
ACCESS: **Paved road, hiking trail** ELEVATION: **4200' - 2800'**
FEATURES: **Suburban wilderness, scenic pools, convenient access**
CAUTIONS: **Weekend crowds, hot summers, steep trails**
MAPS: **USGS -** Sabino Canyon, Mt. Lemmon
   USFS - Coronado National Forest

T his is Tucson's natural playground. Beautiful scenery, picturesque swimming holes, miles of hiking trails and a relaxing atmosphere combine with easy accessibility to make it a very popular recreation site. The area is rich in watchable wildlife. Designated trails and roads provide opportunities for mountain biking and horseback riding.

Nearby Bear Canyon is highlighted by Seven Falls, a popular waterplay and picnicking area. A shuttle bus (fee) provides access to the lower reaches of Sabino Canyon and to the Bear Canyon trailhead. Those who choose, can hike beyond the madding crowds and enjoy comparative solitude farther up canyon. Headwater streams, including Lemmon Creek, offer good trout fishing.

ACCESS: In Tucson, take Speedway to Wilmot to Tanque Verde Road. Turn north off Tanque Verde onto Sabino Canyon Road to the recreation area. You can hike into the Pusch Ridge Wilderness from here.

FACILITIES: There is a visitor center, self-guided nature trail, and picnic areas within the recreation area. Shuttle buses run year-round. USFS developed campgrounds are located along Gen. Hitchcock Road. Other facilities are available in Tucson.

WILDLIFE: Songbirds are plentiful in the canyons. Coyotes, skunks, and mule deer are fairly easy to see. Javelina are more difficult. Bobcats and mountain lions are almost impossible.

CAUTIONS: No pets or glass containers are permitted. Backpackers must hike a quarter mile past the end of the road in Sabino Canyon or past Seven Falls in Bear Canyon before camping. Lower stretches of the stream dry up in summer.

INFORMATION: Coronado National Forest, Santa Catalina Ranger District

USES:

fee

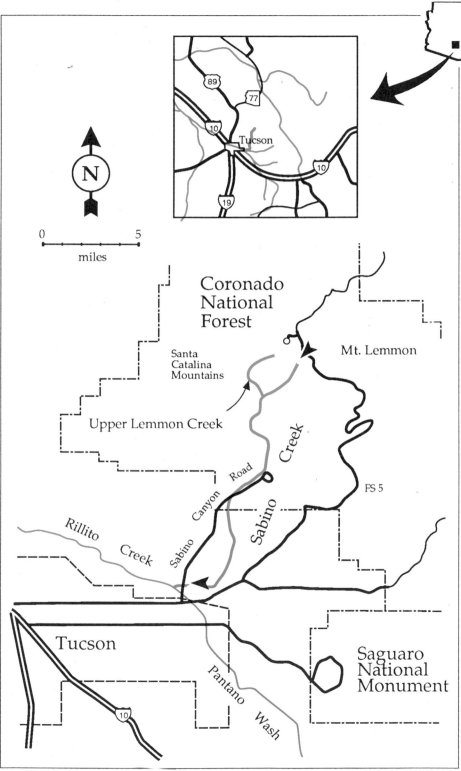

SAN PEDRO RIVER — International
Boundary to Benson

LENGTH: **56 miles**   SEASON: **Perennial flow**
ACCESS: **Paved road**   ELEVATION: **4250' - 3500'**
FEATURES: **Riparian preserve, profuse wildlife, rich history**
CAUTIONS: **Protected area, day use only, no pets**
MAPS: **USGS** -Hereford, Tombstone SE, Fort Huachuca, Fairbank, Land
         USBLM - San Pedro Project

The cottonwood-willow forest that lines the upper reaches of this river is such an outstanding example of one of the rarest and most rapidly disappearing habitats in North America, that 36 miles of it were recently acquired by the US Bureau of Land Management and designated a National Riparian Conservation Area. Its credentials are impressive. Over 350 species of birds, 82 species of mammals, and 47 species of reptiles and amphibians have been counted. Fossils of extinct mammoths, camels and tapirs indicate that the area has been productive for ages. It is the only site on the continent where those remains have been found with evidence that they were hunted by ancient peoples.

The stream itself is a humble one that flows year-round. Most people come here to observe the abundant wildlife, but hiking and horseback riding are also popular. The area offers an excellent interpretive center.

ACCESS: From Sierra Vista a number of roads lead east to the river and the Conservation Area. Other routes that lead to the river are AZ 90, AZ 92, Hereford Road and Charleston Road.

FACILITIES: Primitive camping is permitted on BLM land. There is a visitor contact center 7 miles east of Sierra Vista on AZ 90. Commercial campgrounds and other facilities are available in nearby Sierra Vista.

WILDLIFE: Diversity and uniqueness are the watchwords. Here you may see everything from crested caracaras to green kingfishers to eastern phoebes. Mammals include deer, coyote, kit foxes, coatimundis, bobcats and ringtails.

CAUTIONS: Above all else this is a preserve — recreational activities take a backseat to the welfare of the resource. Some areas are closed to the public. Walk softly.

INFORMATION: USBLM, San Pedro Project Office, Sierra Vista Chamber of Commerce.

USES:
                                              cold   primitive

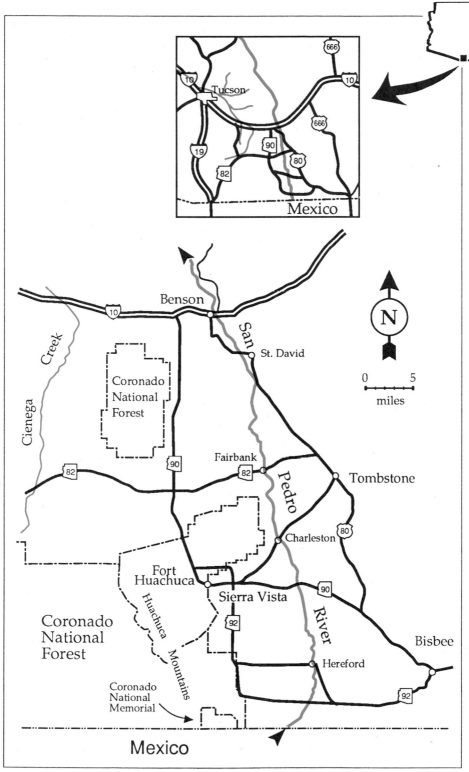

SONOITA CREEK

LENGTH: **8 miles**
ACCESS: **Paved Road**
FEATURES: **Lush riparian area, wildlife sanctuary**
CAUTIONS: **Private land, no camping, picnicking, or pets**
MAPS: **USGS** -Sonoita, Mt. Hughes, Patagonia, Cumero Canyon, Rio Rico

SEASON: **Perennial flow**
ELEVATION: **4100' - 3800'**

Sonoita Creek flows through a high rolling grassland dotted with scrub oaks. The stream itself is bordered by stands cottonwood, willow and mesquite that in some places are exceptionally lush. The Nature Conservancy has set aside one of the best of those areas, near the town of Patagonia, as a wildlife sanctuary. It is widely known as an excellent place for birdwatching and wildlife observation.

Over 200 species of birds have been observed at the preserve, many of them more commonly associated with Mexico. Songbirds are most prevalent within its boundaries, while hawks soar above the oak savannahs outside it. In addition to hiking and birdwatching, hunting and horseback riding are popular along the stream beyond the boundaries of the preserve.

ACCESS: AZ 82 parallels the stream between the town of Sonoita and Nogales. To reach the preserve, turn northwest off AZ 82 in Patagonia on 4th Avenue. Then turn left on Pennsylvania Ave and ford the stream to the preserve.

FACILITIES: There is a developed campground at Patagonia Lake State Park along Sonoita Creek about 10 miles southeast of town. Other facilities are available in Sonoita, Patagonia and Nogales.

WILDLIFE: Look for some really exotic birds here, like thick-billed kingbirds, rose-throated becards, buff-breasted flycatchers, and yellow-billed cuckoos. Also rare gray hawks. Mammals include mule deer and coatimundis.

CAUTIONS: No camping, picnicking, or pets are permitted in the preserve. This preserve was set aside to protect a unique, banishing ecosystem. Walk softly. Much of the land bordering the stream is privately owned.

INFORMATION: USBLM, Tucson Office; The Nature Conservancy, Patagonia-Sonoita Preserve

USES:

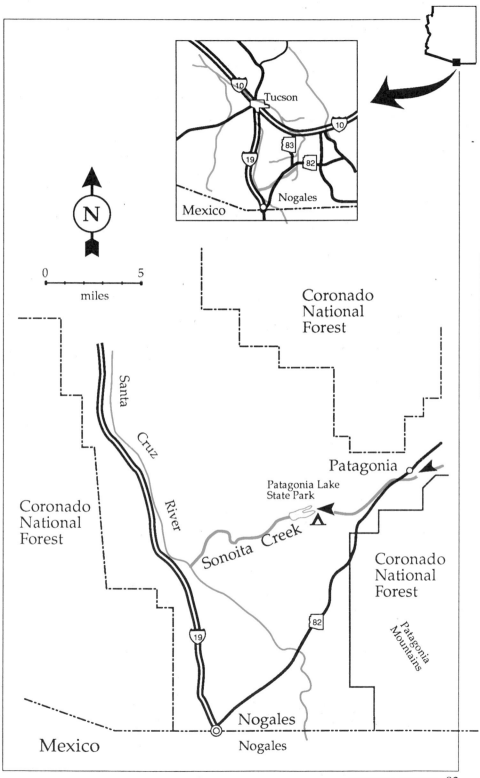

Coronado
National
Forest

Patagonia

Patagonia Lake
State Park

Santa

Cruz

River

Sonoita Creek

Coronado
National
Forest

Coronado
National
Forest

Patagonia
Mountains

Nogales

Mexico

Nogales

Tucson

Mexico

Nogales

SYCAMORE CREEK — In the Pajaritos

LENGTH: **6 miles**   SEASON: **Perennial flow**
ACCESS: **Dirt road, streambed trail**   ELEVATION: **4,000' - 3500'**
FEATURES: **Unique vegetation, scenic stream, watchable wildlife**
CAUTIONS: **Streambed route, narrow canyon, flash floods**
MAPS: **USGS** -Ruby
       USFS - Coronado National Forest

T his pleasant little stream flows into Mexico through a remote canyon highlighted by rare plants, native fish, and colorful birds. Part of this unique area has been set aside as the Goodding Research Natural Area, much of the rest is within a designated Wilderness Area. Over 600 different plant species have been catalogued here. One of those plants reportedly exists only here, in a few other sites in Mexico, and in the Himalayas.

For lack of a trail, hiking in the canyon is limited to the streambed. Streambed hiking is highly inadvisable if there's a chance of a flash flood, but it can be a real delight if the weather is hot and the pools are full. About six miles down canyon you'll run into a fence that marks the Mexican border — a good place to turn around.

ACCESS: About 55 miles south of Tucson, exit I-19 at AZ 289. Drive west 20 miles and turn south at the Sycamore Canyon sign. It's about 0.5 miles to the parking lot and trailhead at Hank and Yank Spring.

FACILITIES: There are a number of primitive campsites at the trailhead. Two USFS campgrounds are located off AZ 289 near Pena Blanca Lake. Other facilities are available along I-19, in Nogales, and in Tucson.

WILDLIFE: Vermilion flycatchers are just one of a number of colorful birds that may be seen here. Watch for coatimundis and their raccoon cousins along the stream. Threatened Sonoran chubs swim in the waters.

CAUTIONS: Don't start down the stream if there's a chance of a flash flood. No camping is permitted along the streambed trail. The trail does require some boulder hopping and wading.

INFORMATION: Coronado National Forest, Nogales Ranger District

USES:

                                              primitive

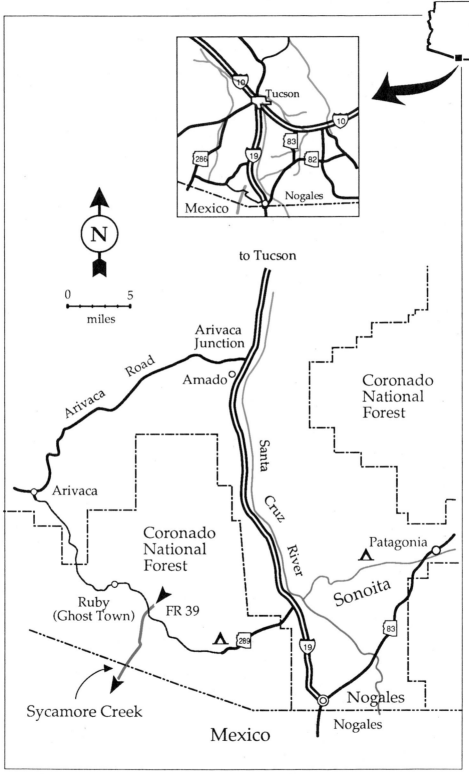

to Tucson

N

0   5
miles

Arivaca Junction

Amado

Arivaca Road

Arivaca

Coronado National Forest

Coronado National Forest

Santa Cruz River

Patagonia

Sonoita

Ruby (Ghost Town)

FR 39

Sycamore Creek

289

19

83

Nogales

Nogales

Mexico

Tucson

Mexico

Nogales

10

10

83

82

19

286

South

Arizona Rivers and Streams Guide

Eastern Section

Big Bonito Creek
Black River
Blue River
Bonita Creek
Canyon Creek
Cherry Creek
Cibeque Creek
Eagle Creek
Gila River
Salt River
San Francisco River
White River

White River—East Fork, by Dan Dagget

BIG BONITO CREEK

LENGTH: **11 miles**　　　　　　SEASON: **Perennial flow**
ACCESS: **Dirt road, hiking trail**　　ELEVATION: **7000' - 5250'**
FEATURES: **Trout fishing, secluded pools**
CAUTIONS: **Reservation permits required, unmarked roads**
MAPS: **USGS** - Odart Mtn, Corn Creek, Bonito Prairie, Elwood Canyon
　　　　USFS - Fort Apache (White Mtn Apache) Reservation

B ig Bonito Creek flows out of the alpine forests and meadows of the
White Mountains, the highest uplands in Arizona. *Bonito* means pretty
in Spanish and the creek lives up to the description. Oak, willow and
cottonwood grow between low canyon walls of black basalt, while open
grasslands stretch back from the rims. The waters of the creek flow clear and
cold over ledges and boulders into pools stocked with trout.

Most people come to Big Bonito Creek to fish, others to hunt the
country that surrounds it. Mountain lion, black bear and javelina are
plentiful here. The White Mountain Apaches have designated the stream's
middle reaches as a special use area and require an additional permit to
enter there. Its upper reaches, which still hold remnant populations of
native trout (*Salmo apache*), are closed.

ACCESS: South of Whiteriver, turn
east off AZ 73 toward Fort Apache.
Follow this paved road past an
elementary school to another
building on the right that looks like
an old one-room school. Turn south
on a road with a stack of signs listing a number of lakes and other recreation sites (but not Big Bonito Ck).
Follow this road to Bonito Creek and
a small campground.

FACILITIES: There are three primitive campsites downstream of the
bridge. Other facilities are available
in Whiteriver.

WILDLIFE: Kestrels soar among
the pinyon and juniper of the grass-

lands above the canyon rims.
Endangered native trout (*Salmo
apache*) live in the upper, closed
stretches. Lower stretches are
stocked with brook and brown trout
with some smallmouth bass near the
confluence with the White River.

CAUTIONS: Instead of an AZ
fishing license, a White Mtn or San
Carlos Apache permit is required.
Above the upper access (listed on
maps as Y70 but unmarked on the
ground), an additional daily special
use permit is required.

INFORMATION: Fort Apache
(White Mtn Apache) Reservation

USES:　　　　　　　　　　
　　　　　　　　　　　　　　cold　　　　　fee

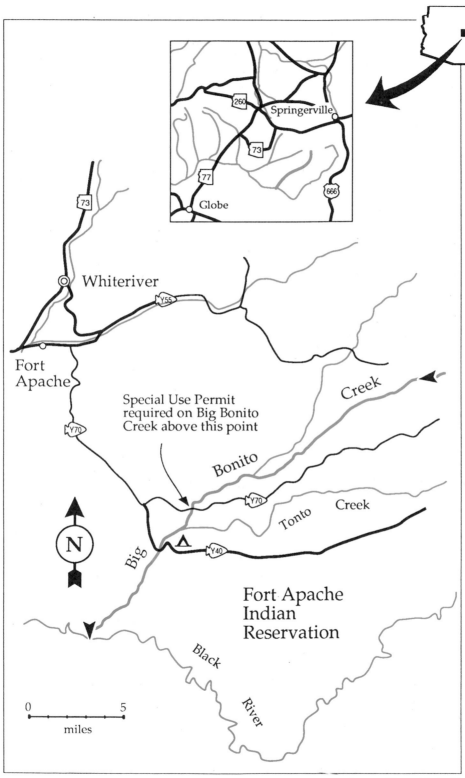

Special Use Permit
required on Big Bonito
Creek above this point

Fort Apache
Indian
Reservation

East

BLACK RIVER—East Fork

LENGTH: **8 miles**   SEASON: **Perennial flow**
ACCESS: **Dirt road, hiking trail**   ELEVATION: **7900' - 7525'**
FEATURES: **Trout fishing, easy access, alpine scenery**
CAUTIONS: **Summer weekend crowds**
MAPS: **USGS** - Rudd Knoll, Buffalo Crossing
      USFS - Apache -Sitgreaves National Forest

I f you were trying to illustrate the incredible diversity you can find among Arizona's streams, this little creek would certainly serve as one of the benchmarks. Flowing past tall pines, willows, and alders, with lush green grass growing right up to its banks, the East Fork could just as easily be in the Rockies of Montana as the White Mountains of Arizona. The outstanding beauty of this stream and the cool weather of its alpine habitat make it an extremely popular summer retreat.

Gone are the days when stringers of fish became so heavy that anglers had trouble carrying them home, but fishing is still quite popular. When not fishing you can ride your bike along the road as it parallels the stream and enjoy just looking at the river. Though it seems impossible, each successive pool always seems a little prettier than the last. Take good care of them.

ACCESS: Just north of Alpine turn west on FR 249 toward Big Lake for 4.5 miles then south on FS 276 to Diamond Rock Campground. Or 6 miles north of Hannagan Meadow, at Beaver Creek, turn west on FR 26 for 10 miles then north on FR 24 for about 3.5 miles to Buffalo Crossing.

FACILITIES: USFS campsites at either end of this stretch and one between Diamond Rock and Buffalo Crossing. Big Lake and Hannagan Meadow have a small store and gas station. Other facilities in Alpine.

WILDLIFE: Elk and wild turkey are plentiful. Abert squirrels scurry through the treetops and Steller's jays raid the garbage cans. So does an occasional black bear. The stream is stocked with trout and dammed by beavers.

CAUTIONS: The campgrounds are closed October through April, but primitive sites remain open, though they might be covered with snow. (Even in summer, nights can be quite chilly here.) Before going to the East Fork, go back to the introduction and read the section on low impact use. This place deserves it.

INFORMATION: Apache-Sitgreaves Nat Forest, Alpine Ranger District

USES:

                                 cold   fee

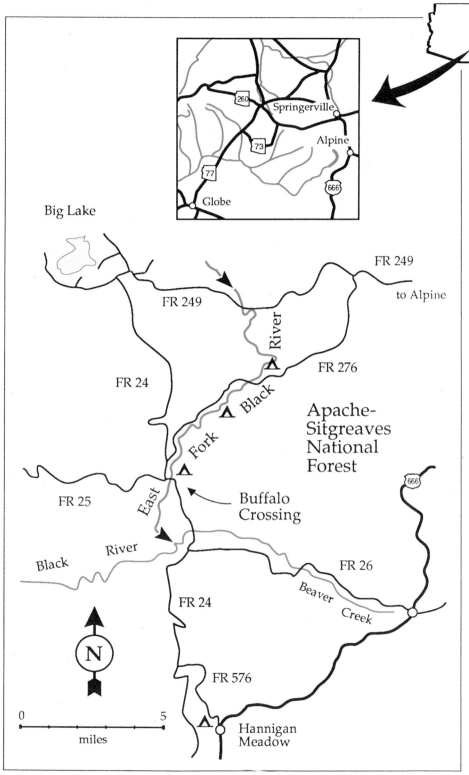

Big Lake

FR 249

to Alpine

FR 276

FR 24

Apache-
Sitgreaves
National
Forest

Black

Fork

River

East

FR 25

Buffalo
Crossing

Black

River

FR 26

Beaver

Creek

FR 24

FR 576

Hannigan
Meadow

N

0   5

miles

260

Springerville

73

Alpine

77

666

Globe

East

BLACK RIVER — West Fork to Reservation Boundary

LENGTH: **8 miles**
ACCESS: **Dirt road, hiking trail**
FEATURES: **Trout fishing, mountain meadows, alpine scenery**
CAUTIONS: **Limited access**
MAPS: **USGS -** Buffalo Crossing, Hannagan Meadow, Hoodoo Knob
   USFS - Apache-Sitgreaves National Forest

SEASON: **Perennial flow**
ELEVATION: **7525' - 6520'**

The East Fork and the West Fork come together to form the Black River in an area of high meadows and alpine forests. Below this, the stream drops through a deep valley as it cuts its way to its confluence with the White River (forming the Salt River). Access along this stretch requires some walking from either the upstream or downstream access points or from spur roads and hiking trails that lead up to the valley's edge.

There is good fishing for stocked trout with some resident fish in more remote areas to entice experienced anglers. Elk, wild turkey and mule deer are common and become less shy as memories of hunting season fade. The bears remain secretive except for the ones made bold by an addiction to garbage. A tribal permit is required to enter the reservation.

ACCESS: Turn west off US 666 onto FR 26 at Beaver Creek, 9 miles north of Hannagan Meadow. Drive 10 miles to FR 24, then north about 3.5 miles to Buffalo Crossing. Take FR 25 west to Wildcat Point.

FACILITIES: There is a USFS developed campsite at Buffalo Crossing and another three miles north of FR 25 on FR 68 along West Fork. A small primitive campsite is available at the Wildcat Point bridge. There is a gas station and small store at Big Lake and Hannagan Meadow. Other facilities are available in Alpine.

WILDLIFE: Elk, wild turkey and black bear are plentiful here. Abert's squirrels, Steller's jays, and beavers are commonly seen small animals. The stream is stocked with rainbow trout.

CAUTIONS: The campgrounds are closed October through April. Primitive sites remain open, though they may be accessible only by skis. Even summer nights can be quite chilly here. Keep a clean camp to avoid creating problem bears.

INFORMATION: Apache-Sitgreaves National Forest, Alpine Ranger District

USES:

cold   fee

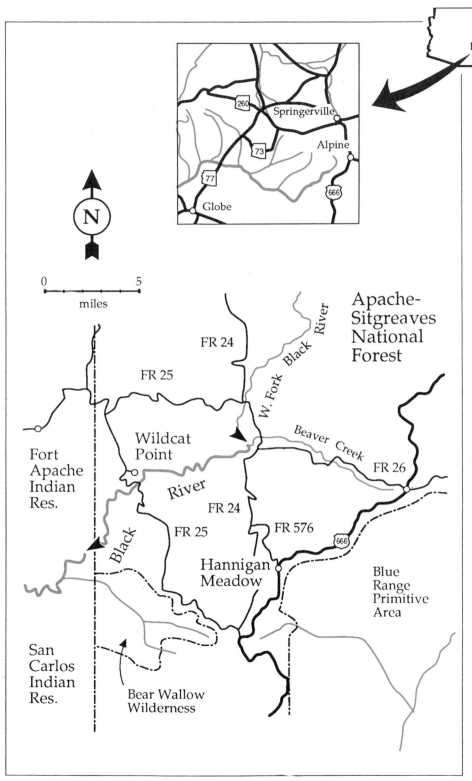

BLACK RIVER — Reservation Boundary to White Confluence

LENGTH: **45 miles** SEASON: **Perennial flow**
ACCESS: **Dirt road, hiking trail** ELEVATION: **6520' - 4400'**
FEATURES: **Famous smallmouth bass fishing, alpine scenery**
CAUTIONS: **Limited access, reservation permit required**
MAPS: **USGS** - (1:100,000) Nutrioso, Clifton, Showlow
 USBIA - White Mtn Apache Indian Res, San Carlos Indian Res.

After leaving the Apache-Sitgreaves National Forest, the Black River forms the boundary between the White Mountain and San Carlos Indian reservations. A fishing permit and a daily special use permit from either tribe is required to enter this area. No Arizona State fishing license is needed and having one is no substitute for a reservation permit.

This part of the river is famous for its excellent smallmouth bass fishing. Smallmouth are cool water fish known for the excitement they provide on the business end of a fishing line. The best fishing is in secluded pools away from road access points. Access is by several reservation roads, some unmarked. Get a map from the tribal game and fish department, available at most stores on the reservation, then ask directions. This stream looks boatable in places but the Apaches haven't opened it to that activity.

ACCESS: South of Whiteriver, turn east off AZ 73 toward Fort Apache. Take this paved road past an elementary school to another building on the right that looks like an old one-room school. Turn south onto a road with a stack of signs listing a number of lakes and other recreation sites. Several roads branch off this main road down to the river.

FACILITIES: There is a campground at Black River Crossing on reservation Rt 9 and another on a spur off Rt 9 that leads south after crossing the White River. Some primitive campsites are located at other road access points to the river.

WILDLIFE: Elk, wild turkey and mule deer are common. Black bears roam the forests and oak thickets, and beavers swim in the stream, which is home to Arizona's largest population of smallmouth bass.

CAUTIONS: The roads are poorly marked. Use an official reservation game and fish department map, ask directions. A White Mtn or San Carlos Apache fishing permit and a daily special use permit (needed for all activities) are required to fish.

INFORMATION: White Mountain Apache Indian Reservation; San Carlos Indian Reservation

USES:

 fee cool fee fee fee

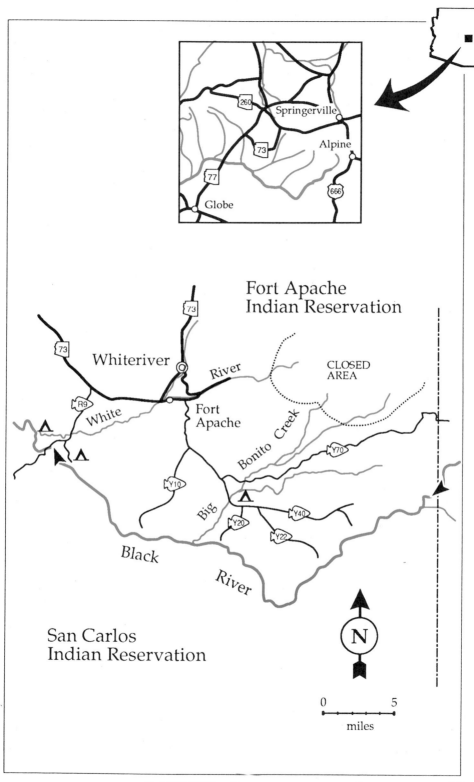

East

BLUE RIVER — Blue Crossing to FR 475

LENGTH: **24 miles**
ACCESS: **Dirt road, hiking trail**
FEATURES: **Primitive area, secluded canyon**
CAUTIONS: **Low flows, limited access, private property**
MAPS: **USGS -** Blue, Bear Mtn, Dutch Blue Creek, Fritz Canyon, Dix Creek
 USFS - Apache-Sitgreaves National Forest

SEASON: **Early March**
ELEVATION: **5250' - 4200'**

O nce in a blue moon this little stream gets enough snow melt to be boatable. That doesn't make it any less notable. The streambed provides an access route into the largest roadless area left in the Southwest. Officially, this is a primitive area, which means it is a wilderness in virtually every way but local designation.

A single streamside road offers access to this remote country, and if you want to explore beyond it you'll have to walk... or wait for a blue moon float trip. You can hike when you can't boat, but you might have to swim. In places, the canyon walls come right to the streambanks. People fish the Blue, too. Below that it's catfish and maybe a smallmouth bass or two. The few people who have floated this river say it's an experience worth waiting for.

ACCESS: <u>Upper</u>: From Alpine take US 180 east to Luna Lake then south 23 miles on FR 281 to Blue Crossing and 14 miles to the end of the road where the few people who have run this stretch launched their boats. <u>Lower</u>: Drive north 21 miles from Morenci on US 666, then east on FR 475.

FACILITIES: USFS campgrounds at Blue Crossing, a few miles upstream at Upper Blue and two along FR 475 just east of US 666. Other facilities in Clifton and Morenci.

WILDLIFE: The Blue area is so remote and so wild that there has been talk of reintroducing grizzly

bears here. Until then, you'll have to make do with black bears and mountain lions, mule deer, elk, and javelina. The riparian area attracts a large number of songbirds, and it's a good place to see hummingbirds.

CAUTIONS: Respect private property boundaries. People like their privacy down here. If you do get a chance to boat the stream, watch out for everything from fences and logjams to abandoned farm machinery.

INFORMATION: Apache-Sitgreaves National Forest, Clifton and Alpine Ranger Districts

USES:

Class I & II   cold

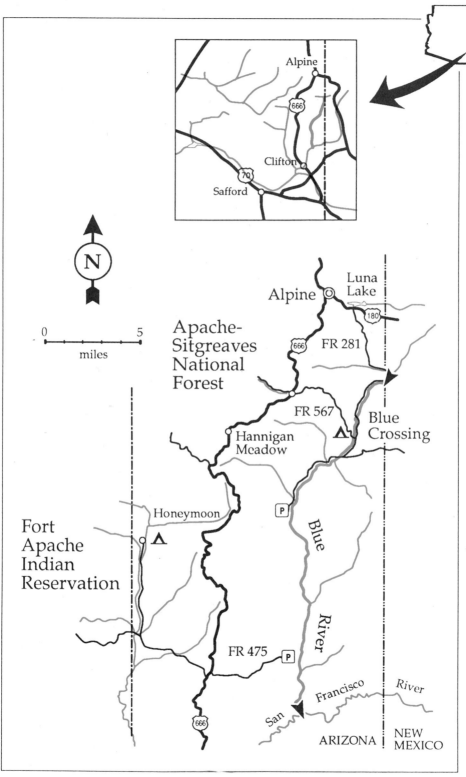

Alpine

Clifton

70

Safford

N

0   5
miles

Apache-
Sitgreaves
National
Forest

Alpine   Luna
Lake

666   FR 281

180

FR 567

Blue
Crossing

Hannigan
Meadow

Honeymoon

Fort
Apache
Indian
Reservation

P

Blue

P

River

FR 475

666

San   Francisco   River

ARIZONA | NEW
MEXICO

BONITA CREEK — Reservation Boundary to Gila Confluence

LENGTH: **19 miles**
ACCESS: **Dirt road (HCV)**
FEATURES: **Rare raptors, scenic canyon, easy access**
CAUTIONS: **Low flows, ORV damage**
MAPS: **USGS** - (1:100,000) Nutrioso, Clifton, Showlow
      USBLM - Safford District

SEASON: **Perennial flow**
ELEVATION: **4400' -3150'**

Bonita Creek is unique in a number of ways. It provides habitat for a variety of raptors. It roughly marks the western limit of Rocky Mountain bighorn sheep colonization in Arizona (wild sheep to the west are desert bighorns), and in and around this narrow, steep canyon the Sonoran and Chihuahuan deserts intermingle to form a unique plant community.

With a road running up the canyon bottom, Bonita Creek (Spanish for pretty) is an easily accessible place for people to picnic under its cottonwoods and splash in its shallow pools and riffles. Bird watching is another favorite activity, made rewarding by the variety and rarity of the species that can be seen here. And the creek itself contains some rare native fish. In recognition of its outstanding characteristics, Bonita Creek has been nominated for inclusion in Arizona's Unique Waters system.

ACCESS: Drive 7 miles west out of Safford on US 70, turn north for 6 miles on the San Jose Road to the City of Safford Utility Road. Turn east and follow this road down to the creek and the HCV road that leads up canyon.

FACILITIES: There are some primitive campsites located along the road that parallels the river. Other facilities are available in Safford.

WILDLIFE: A number of rare raptors frequent the area, including zone-tailed hawks and threatened Mexican black hawks. This is one of the few places in Arizona where you can see Rocky Mountain bighorn sheep. The stream is home to two threatened fish species, the spike-dace and the loach minnow.

CAUTIONS: The road up Bonita Creek Canyon is classified as suitable for HCV's and 4WD's. The area has suffered ORV damage. Watch out for flash floods if you camp in the canyon.

INFORMATION: U. S. Bureau of Land Management, Safford District; Safford Chamber of Commerce

USES:

primitive raptors

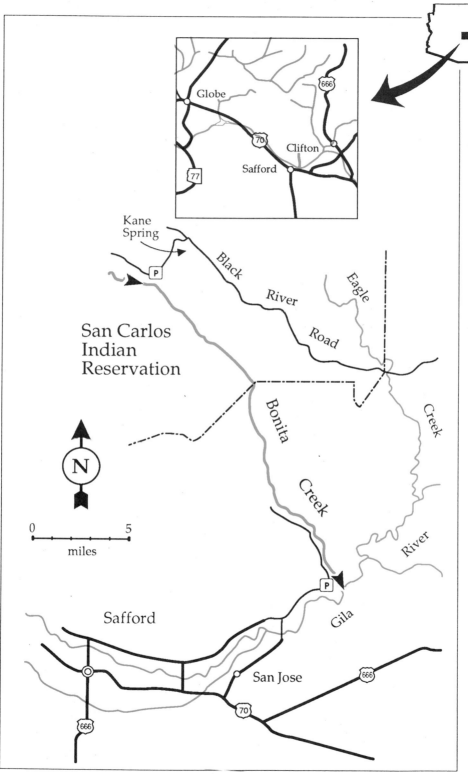

East

CANYON CREEK

LENGTH: **31 miles**

SEASON: **Perennial flow**

ACCESS: **Dirt road (HCV)**

ELEVATION: **5300' - 2905'**

FEATURES: **Scenic area, excellent trout fishing**

CAUTIONS: **Indian reservation, dual regulation, restricted fishing**

MAPS: **USGS -** (1:100,000) Woods Canyon, Young, Chediski Peak, Blue House Mtn.

USFS - Tonto Natl. Forest, Fort Apache (White Mtn.) Indian Reserv.

K nown as one of the best trout streams in the state, it springs into existence under the Mogollan Rim on the Tonto National Forest. This is a beautiful stream in a unique setting. If you don't fish, it's a good place to hike and watch the abundant wildlife. The creek spans so many life zones that hiking its length is equivalent to traveling from Canada to Mexico. The lower portions of the stream are accessible from the Salt River.

On National Forest land an Arizona fishing license and the use of artificial lures only are required. Stream access and campgrounds are common. On the Apache side, both a tribal fishing license and a daily special use permit (necessary for all activities) are required.

ACCESS: East of Payson turn south off AZ 260 onto FR 512, then west at the Rim on FR 33. Additional access via FR 33 to FR 34 to FR 188. On the White Mtn Apache side, turn west off US 60 north of the Salt River Canyon Bridge on Indian Service Rt 12 to Cibeque. Take RR O21 out of Cibeque past Grasshopper to Canyon Ck.

FACILITIES: USFS campgrounds at Airplane Flat and Canyon Ck on FR 33. The Apaches permit camping along the creek at Iron Mine and Chediski Farms. Other facilities at Payson, Globe and Cibeque. Reservation permits may be purchased at the Salt River Bridge-US 60 store and the Cibeque Commercial Center.

WILDLIFE: Black bear and elk to javelina and road runners. The upper reaches support a number of interesting forest species including Abert squirrels.

CAUTIONS: Be sure to have all the appropriate permits. The roads are not always marked; finding your way through the Reservation requires an intuitive sense of direction and an ability to ask questions and follow directions (a few places are off limits).

INFORMATION: Tonto National Forest, Pleasant Valley Ranger Dist; Fort Apache Reservation

USES:

cold

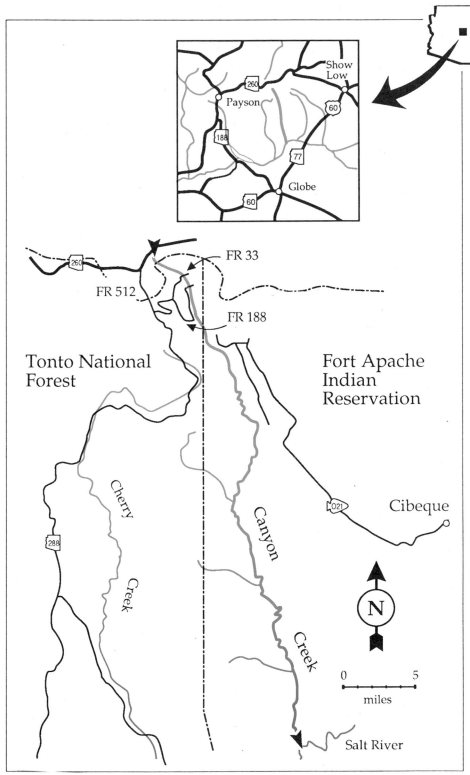

Show
Low

Payson

Globe

FR 33

FR 512

FR 188

Tonto National
Forest

Fort Apache
Indian
Reservation

Cherry

Canyon

Creek

Cibeque

Creek

N

0   5

miles

Salt River

East

CHERRY CREEK

LENGTH: **45 miles**

SEASON: **Perennial flow**

ACCESS: **Paved road/dirt road**

ELEVATION: **6400' - 2450'**

FEATURES: **Historic site, wild country, scenic canyon**

CAUTIONS: **Flash Floods, HCV access, low flows in summer**

MAPS: **USGS -** (1:100,000) Young, McFadden Peak, Rockinstraw Mtn.

   USFS - Tonto National Forest, Pleasant Valley Ranger District

C herry Creek flows out of Pleasant Valley, the site of what may have been Arizona's most violent range war-the Pleasant Valley War, a deadly feud between two frontier clans in the late nineteenth century. The creek itself is small and sometimes nearly dry. However, it still provides valuable recreation for those who like to camp in its side canyons and swim or wade in its deeper pools. Its headwaters are near the town of Young, which has been described as Arizona's last cow town.

After leaving Pleasant Valley, the creek drops through a rugged canyon, flowing from upper to lower Sonoran desert life zones, then enters the Salt River Canyon Wilderness. The creek supports a rich riparian area, including tall cottonwoods and sycamores, that attracts a variety of colorful songbirds as well as raptors and herons.

ACCESS: Cherry Creek Road (FR 203) turns east off AZ 288 just north of the Salt River Bridge. It parallels the stream into Cherry Creek Canyon. Access to the northern portion of the stream is via FR 54 out of Young.

FACILITIES: There are a few primitive campsites along the stream off FR 203. Two USFS developed campgrounds are located along AZ 288 several miles beyond the Cherry Creek cutoff. Young hosts some colorful old restaurants, bars and grocery stores. Other facilities available in Globe.

WILDLIFE: Look for javelina, coatimundi, gila monsters, bobcat, lots of mule deer and mountain lion. Colorful birds like hooded orioles, vermillion flycatchers and yellow warblers light up the cottonwoods.

CAUTIONS: Watch out for flash floods. Respect the private property rights of the residents. FR 203 is recommended for high clearance vehicles only.

INFORMATION: Tonto National Forest, Pleasant Valley District

USES:

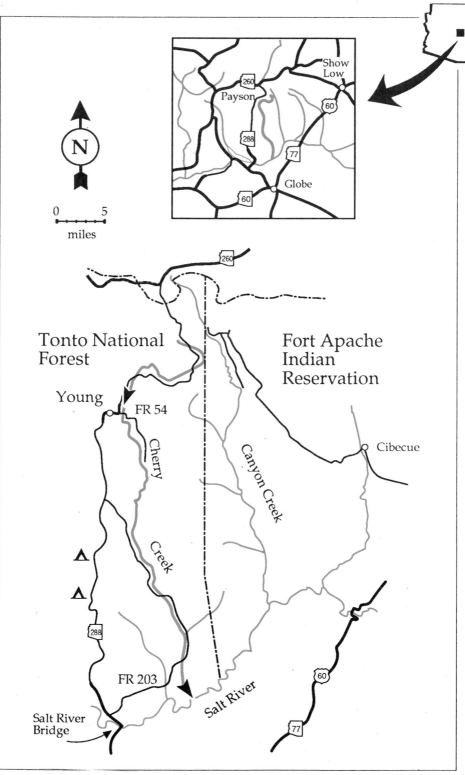

CIBEQUE CREEK

LENGTH: **20 miles**
ACCESS: **Dirt road**
SEASON: **Perennial flow**
ELEVATION: **5680' - 3136'**
FEATURES: **Scenic area, trout fishing, waterfalls**
CAUTIONS: **Indian reservation, fee area, steep trail**
MAPS: **USGS -** Pepper Canyon, Spotted Mtn, Cibeque, Cibeque Peak, Blue House Mtn, Mule Hoof Bend or (1:100,000) Show Low, Seneca
USFS - Tonto Natl Forest, Fort Apache (White Mtn) Indian Reserv.

Entirely within the White Mountain Apache Reservation, its waters drop 4,400 ft from the crest of the Mogollon Rim to the creek's confluence with the Salt River deep in the Salt River Canyon. Along the way this small stream flows through a deep gorge with thickly forested slopes, a wide valley of neatly kept Apache farms, then a final stairstep plunge to the Salt. The upper reaches are stocked with trout by the Apaches. (Fishing requires a reservation fishing license and a daily special-use permit.)

Below the town of Cibeque, access is limited to walking upstream from the creek's confluence with the Salt. There are a number of waterfalls along this stretch, some of which are quite impressive. This area is popular for hiking and playing in the spray and pools below the falls.

ACCESS: Turn west off US 60 north of the Salt River Bridge on Indian Service Route 12. Follow the signs past the Cibeque Commercial Center, turn right at the stop sign, left at the Assembly of God Church, and right at the next fork in the road. RR O20 parallels the stream for several miles. Lower Cibeque: turn west just beyond the Salt River Bridge and go about 3 mi. on Rt. G1.

FACILITIES: Permits are required for the primitive campsites along the creek just above Rt. O20 and the two primitive campgrounds along Rt. G1 between the Salt River bridge and the mouth of Cibeque Creek.

WILDLIFE: Upper Cibeque is home to elk, deer, bear and Abert squirrels. The middle stretch harbors warblers and other songbirds while hawks and turkey vultures soar above. Downstream are javelina, ringtail cats and colorful songbirds. Trout in the upper reaches; catfish and smallmouth bass below.

CAUTIONS: Some kind of permit is required just to drive off the paved roads and/or get out of your car. The roads are not always marked — finding your way can be quite a challenge.

INFORMATION: White Mountain Apache Reservation

USES:

cold · fee

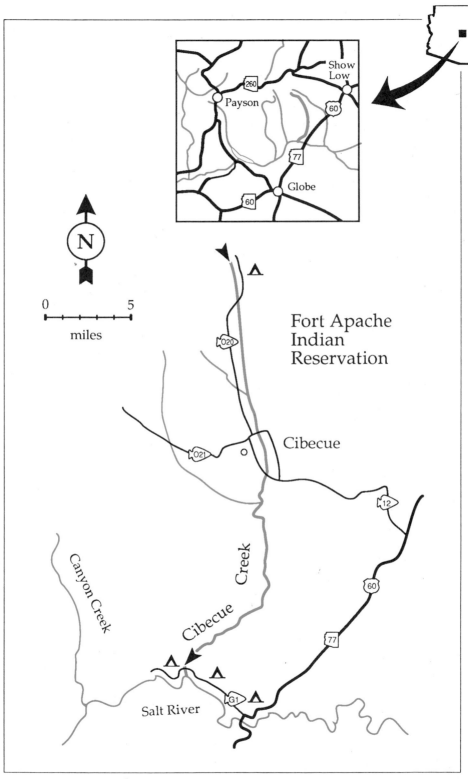

EAGLE CREEK

LENGTH: **48 miles**   SEASON: **Perennial flow**
ACCESS: **Dirt road (HCV)**   ELEVATION: **5450' - 3250'**
FEATURES: **Rare raptors, scenic canyon, easy access**
CAUTIONS: **Low flows, ORV damage, private property**
MAPS: **USGS** - (1:100,000) Safford, Clifton, Nutrioso
      USBLM - Safford District

E agle Creek is one of the best places in the state to see a variety of hawks and other raptors, including the Mexican black hawk. This critical nesting area has been estimated to host 10% of the U. S. population of this rare species. Other raptors include zone-tailed hawks, endangered peregrine falcons, and wintering bald eagles.

From its source in the White Mountains to its end at the Gila River, the stream criss-crosses the boundary between the Apache-Sitgreaves National Forest and the San Carlos Indian Reservation. Much of the land bordering it is private, especially along the last twisting miles above the Gila, the most notable raptor habitat. While these lower stretches are popular with birders, upstream areas are bettter known for hiking and fishing.

ACCESS: Drive north on US 666 through Clifton and Morenci. Just before an overlook of the open pit mine, turn left at a sign marking the road to lower Eagle Creek. From 666 north of Morenci follow FR 217 to upper Eagle Creek. Trail #13 leads to a middle stretch of the creek from 666 just within the Forest boundary.

FACILITIES: There are USFS developed campgrounds along upper Eagle Creek at Honeymoon, and along US 666. Other facilities in Clifton and Morenci.

WILDLIFE: Threatened Mexican black hawks nest here in large numbers. Endangered peregrine falcons can also be seen. The threatened spikedace and the loach minnow swim in the lower reaches of the stream, trout in the upper reaches. Rocky Mountain bighorn sheep have spread into the area.

CAUTIONS: Much of the land along middle Eagle Creek is on the San Carlos Apache Reservation. Appropriate permits are required. Lower Eagle Creek is owned by Phelps Dodge mining company. At present they do not limit access.

INFORMATION: USBLM, Safford District; Apache-Sitgreaves National Forest, Clifton Ranger District; San Carlos Apache Indian Reservation; Phelps Dodge Company

USES:

                      cold   fee   raptors

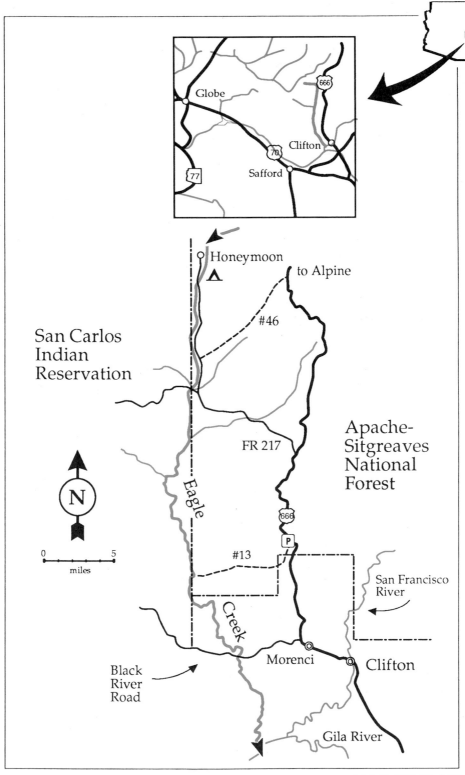

Globe

666

Clifton

70

Safford

77

Honeymoon

to Alpine

#46

San Carlos
Indian
Reservation

FR 217

Apache-
Sitgreaves
National
Forest

Eagle

N

0   5
miles

666

P

#13

San Francisco
River

Creek

Black
River
Road

Morenci

Clifton

Gila River

GILA RIVER — US 666 Bridge to Bonita Creek

LENGTH: **24 miles**
ACCESS: **Paved road, dirt road**
FEATURES: **Scenic canyon, rare hawks, boatable stream**
CAUTIONS: **Short season, fences, private property**
MAPS: **USGS** - York, Guthrie, Gila Box
      USBLM - Safford District

SEASON: **Mid- February — April**
ELEVATION: **3475' -3130'**

This stretch is best known for its dramatic scenery and the rich wildlife community it supports. Downstream of US 666, cliffs rise so abruptly along the river's edge that they form a gorge called the 'Gila Box.' The Box is a popular stretch with river runners. Most years it has a rafting season, albeit a short one. Low water boaters are extending this season.

Though the canyon is dramatic, the river within it has only a few mild rapids. Boaters with less developed skills and less specialized equipment routinely make this run. It's also a good place to see hawks and eagles — strays from Eagle Creek which hosts one of the most diverse raptor communities in the Southwest. Because of its remote character, impressive scenery, and unique wildlife, the Gila Box has been nominated as a wilderness area and has been recommended for study as a possible National Park. If you can't boat it, wait until it's low and hike it — it's worth the trip.

ACCESS: Upper: Driving north into Clifton on US 666 the road splits into four lanes. After the four lanes merge into two the Old Safford Hwy branches to the west and leads to an old bridge. Lower: Drive 7 miles west out of Safford on US 70, north on the San Jose Road 6 miles, then east on the City of Safford Utility Road and down Bonita Creek Road.

FACILITIES: Some primitive campsites at the Old Safford Hwy Bridge and along Bonita Creek. Limited facilities in nearby towns.

WILDLIFE: Some 14 species listed as threatened, endangered, in

jeopardy, or candidates for those designations have been identified here — threatened Mexican black hawks, endangered peregrine falcons, threatened spikedace and loach minnow. Rocky Mountain bighorn sheep have spread into the area from New Mexico.

CAUTIONS: At low water two fences can be life threatening obstacles just below the put-in. Private property borders the river at some spots. It should be avoided.

INFORMATION: US BLM, Safford District Office.

USES:
Class I-II

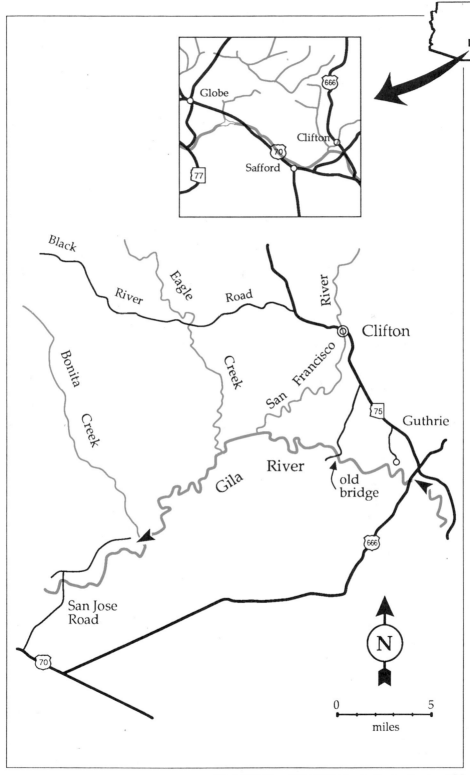

Black River

Eagle

Road

River

Clifton

Bonita Creek

Creek

San Francisco

75

Guthrie

Gila River

old bridge

666

San Jose Road

70

Globe

70

Clifton

Safford

77

666

N

East

0   5

miles

GILA RIVER — Coolidge Dam to Winkelman

LENGTH: 10 miles
ACCESS: Dirt road, paved road
FEATURES: Wild canyon, desert river
CAUTIONS: Lethal logjams, cold water, remoteness, strainers, hot summer heat
MAPS: USGS - Christmas, Hayden, Winkelman
　　　　USBLM/BIA - BLM, Phoenix District; San Carlos Apache Reserv.

SEASON: Perennial flow
ELEVATION: 2350' - 1900'

G ila River boating offers a way to enjoy a ten-mile section of Gila River upstream from Winkelman. This float has gentle rapids, except during flooding periods. Canoes, kayaks, and small rafts can do the river in two to three hours, depending on put-in, flow, and winds. Trees and other hazards make tubing and boating dangerous.

The Gila flows all summer due to releases from Coolidge Dam. The boating season lasts about March to August. Put-in points may require high-clearance, four-wheel-drive vehicles. No permit is needed if you start near Christmas on BLM land for a six-mile trip. If you have a state recreation permit, you can put in near Dripping Springs for a ten-mile run.

ACCESS: From Globe take Hwy 77, 25 miles south to Dripping Springs. Take-out is normally at the park in Winkelman. (Needles Eye Wilderness farther upstream has no public land or river access.) Several companies offer raft trips. Contact Tucson BLM for a complete list of Outfitters. Permits are required.

FACILITIES: There is a developed campground off Rt 3 on San Carlos Lake (reservation permit required). Gas, groceries and permits are available at the San Carlos Marina. Other facilities in Peridot and Globe.

WILDLIFE: There is a herd of elk that was stranded years ago while being transported to the mountains to replenish hunted-out herds. They are referred to as Arizona's desert elk because they live at a lower elevation than any others in the state. Other animals include javelina, mule deer, eagles and osprey.

CAUTIONS: Numerous log-jams and strainers make this stream extremely dangerous - life threatening. Because of its remoteness rescue is sometimes impossible. This is not a boating or tubing area.

INFORMATION: USBLM, Tucson Field Office; San Carlos Apache Indian Res; Gila County SO, Hayden

USES:　　　　　

　　　　　　　　　　　　　　warm　　　　　　　fee　　eagles

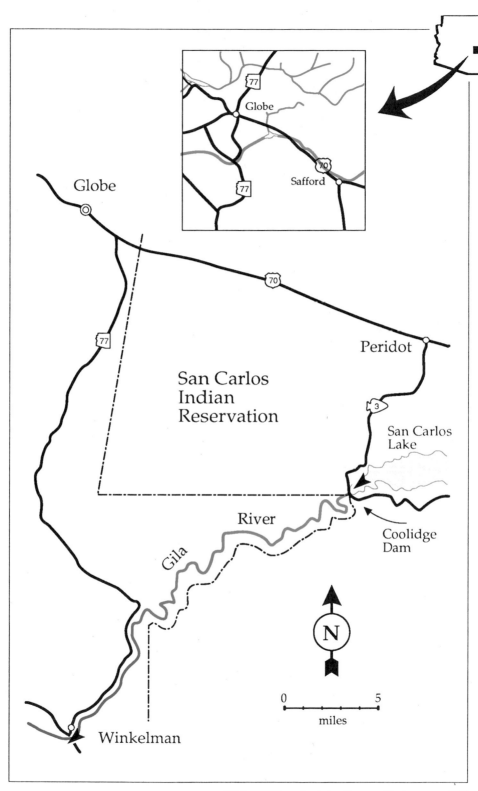

GILA RIVER — Kelvin to Ashurst-Hayden Dam

LENGTH: **19 miles** SEASON: **May-September**
ACCESS: **Paved road** ELEVATION: **1750' - 1575'**
FEATURES: **Extreme remoteness, flowing water**
CAUTIONS: **Lethal log-jams, cold water, extreme remoteness**
MAPS: **USGS -** Kearny, Grayback, North Butte
      USBLM - Tucson Field Office

B elow Kelvin, the Gila River loses some of the nastiness that character-
izes it between Coolidge Dam and Winkelman. There are still logjams
and branches stretched over the water, but they're not as common nor
as dangerous as upstream. The drive to Kelvin, past mile after mile of copper
mines and tailings piles, certainly doesn't promise much scenic beauty, but
on the river all that changes. The riparian area is extremely lush, full of
cottonwoods, willows and mesquite, reminding some people of tropical
rivers. Back from the stream are rolling hills covered with the cactuses and
scrub of the Sonoran Desert.

Boaters who have run this stretch recommend using small inflatabales
instead of canoes because of the former's tendency to bend around limbs and
snags rather than break. If you've got time to fish in between dodging limbs
and spotting birds, there are some catfish and bass.

ACCESS: Upper: Drive south out of
Superior 17 miles on AZ 177 and
turn east toward Kelvin. The road
leads to a bridge across the river.
Lower: Drive south and west out of
Kelvin on the old Florence highway.
About 14 miles out of town the road
passes some large boulders on the
north side. Turn north on a graded
road here and follow the main route
of travel about 6 miles to the river.

FACILITIES: There is a developed
campground east of Superior along
US 60 at Oak Flat. Cochran has
primitive campsites along the stream
at the take out.

WILDLIFE: Boaters report seeing
great horned owls. Songbirds are
plentiful in the riparian canopy
during spring and summer.
Redtailed and Harris' hawks soar
above.

CAUTIONS: Watch out for logjams
and strainers. Releases from
Coolidge Dam are sometimes
erratic. During winter the river can
be very low as water is stored
behind the dam for the summer
irrigation season.

INFORMATION: USBLM Tucson
Field Office; Pinal County Sheriff's
Office, Florence

USES:
Class I & II warm

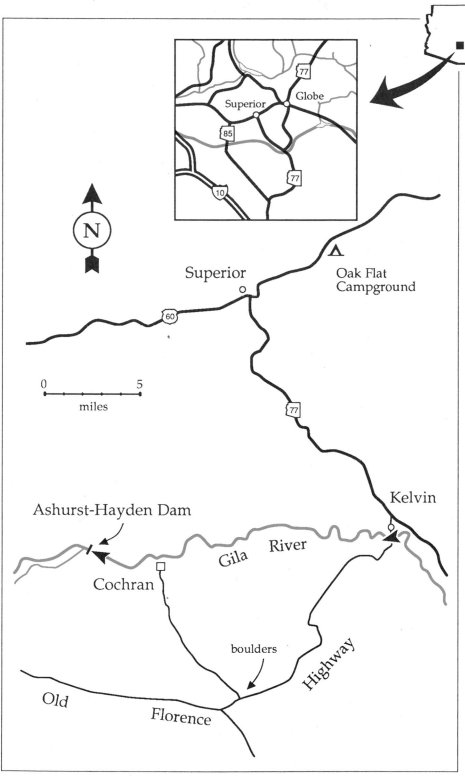

SALT RIVER — US 60 to Gleason Flats

LENGTH: **19.7 miles**
ACCESS: **Paved road/dirt road (HCV)**
FEATURES: **Exciting white water, scenic desert surroundings**
CAUTIONS: **Difficult access, remote conditions, technical rapids**
MAPS: **USGS** - Mule Hoof Bend, Picacho Colorado
    USFS - Tonto National Forest visitor's map, Recreation Opportunity
    Guide.

SEASON: **March & April**
ELEVATION: **3350' - 2840'**

This stretch, and the one downstream, combine to make up Arizona's most technical white water run. The rapids are exciting and complex. They should be run only by experienced boatmen or, at low water, under the guidance of a professional. The big-water rafting season is short, generally from early March to late April. Recently, however, commercial trips have begun running this stretch in small inflatables at low levels. Using this technique they have managed to extend the season.

This stretch of the river flows through upper Sonoran Desert habitat with Indian land on one side and Forest Service land on the other. The Fort Apache Tribe requires a daily permit that serves for boating and camping.

ACCESS: Upper: Take US 60 north out of Globe 40 miles to the Salt River Bridge. Lower: From the Salt River Bridge, drive 19.4 miles down Fort Apache Indian Reservation Road #1, then left on RR #4 for 4.1 miles, right 0.2 miles and left to the river. Alternate access is available at Cibeque Creek and Salt Banks. Or (for 4WD's) turn left off US 60 at the Jones Water Campground onto FR 303, drive 13.5 miles then left on 303A, and left again on 303B, 4 miles to the river.

FACILITIES: There are primitive camps at Mule Hoof near the US 60 Bridge and at Exhibition, 3.3 miles in. Other facilities are available along US 60 and in Globe.

WILDLIFE: Javelina and black bear are seen frequently along this stretch. A number of different bird species inhabit the riparian area. Osprey and eagles soar above it.

CAUTIONS: The rapids are complex and hazardous. Flow levels vary greatly. When in doubt, scout. All unpaved access roads can be impassable when wet. A permit is required from the Fort Apache Tribe for each day on the river. Permits available at the store at AZ 60 Bridge.

INFORMATION: Tonto National Forest; White Mountain Game & Fish Dept.

USES:

Class III+   warm

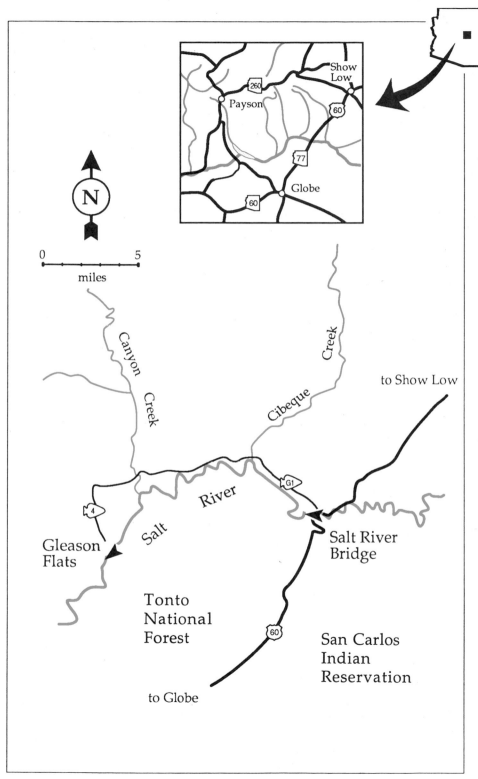

to Show Low

Canyon Creek

Cibeque Creek

River

G1

Salt

4

Gleason
Flats

Salt River
Bridge

Tonto
National
Forest

60

San Carlos
Indian
Reservation

to Globe

Show Low

260

Payson

60

77

Globe

60

East

SALT RIVER — Gleason Flats to Horseshoe Bend

LENGTH: 19.1 miles
ACCESS: Dirt road (HCV)
FEATURES: **Exciting whitewater, scenic desert surroundings**
CAUTIONS: **Many technical rapids, difficult access**
MAPS: **USGS -** Picacho Colorado, Haystack Butte, Dagger Peak
     USFS - Tonto National Forest visitors map

SEASON: March & April
ELEVATION: 2840' - 2400'

D ifficult rapids continue and should only be attempted by experienced river runners or with a commercial guide. At high water it can be deadly. The Forest Service restricts the number of people entering the Wilderness each day. Applications are accepted from Dec. 1- Jan 31.

The rafting season is short, generally lasting from early March through April. However, experienced paddlers using small inflatables have made this run in nearly all months of the year. The surroundings are upper Sonoran Desert. The Tonto National Forest has a detailed guide available for the upper Salt River.

ACCESS: Upper: Follow FR 203 east from AZ 288 (just north of the Salt River Bridge) for 14.9 mi. then right on FR 96 until it becomes Reservation Road #1. Follow it 2.2 mi. then right on RR #3 for 3.9 miles and right again 0.5 miles to the river. Lower: From Globe follow AZ 88 north 6.3 miles. Turn right onto Hicks Drive for two miles, then right on FR 219 for 8 miles. River access is down a steep trail around private land.

FACILITIES: People camp on the river bank at Gleason Flats. There are developed facilities along US 60, in Globe, and in other nearby towns.

WILDLIFE: Javelina and other desert animals are seen along this

stretch. One river runner reports waking up in the morning here to find mountain lion tracks around his bed.

CAUTIONS: Many rapids deserve your respect, especially Corkscrew, just below Quartzite; Black Rock and The Maze. The daily permit required from the Fort Apache Tribe for using their land is available at the store at the AZ 60 Bridge. Group size is limited to 15 within the USFS wilderness.

INFORMATION: White Mtn. Game & Fish Dept. (for permits); Tonto National Forest (for river guide permit applications)

USES:

Class III-V   warm

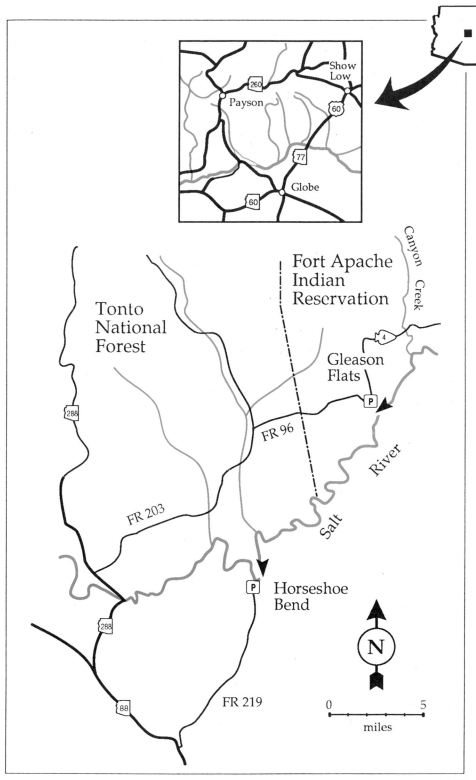

Show Low

260

Payson

60

77

Globe

60

Fort Apache
Indian
Reservation

Canyon Creek

Tonto
National
Forest

4

Gleason
Flats

P

288

FR 96

River

FR 203

Salt

P Horseshoe
Bend

288

N

FR 219

88

0   5
miles

East

SALT RIVER — Horseshoe Bend to Diversion Dam

LENGTH: **13.8 miles**   SEASON: **March-April** *inconsistent*
ACCESS: **Dirt road/paved road**   ELEVATION: **2400' - 2200'**
FEATURES: **Long season, scenic desert surroundings, desert bald eagles**
CAUTIONS: **Wildlife closure, diversion dam (unrunnable)**
MAPS: **USGS -** Dagger Peak, Windy Hill, Roosevelt Dam
      USFS - Tonto National Forest visitor's map, Recreation Opportunity
      Guide-Upper Salt River

B elow Horseshoe Bend the canyon broadens and its rapids mellow. The river is more like a frisky spring colt than the rodeo bull it resembles upstream. Though the rafting season is limited to March and April, this stretch can be run by low water boaters year-round. Access to this portion of the Wilderness is restricted by the Forest Service. Applications accepted Dec. 1-Jan. 31.

The Sonoran desert vegetation is exceptionally lush in this area. Giant saguaro cactuses dot the slopes that rise from the river. The riparian area serves as home to a pair of southern (desert) bald eagles, one of only twenty-six nesting pairs in the world (no stopping near their nest).

The 288 Bridge River Access Point is the last place to take out.

ACCESS: Upper: From Globe-Miami, follow AZ 88 north 6.3 miles. Turn right onto Hicks Drive for two miles then right on FR 219 for 8 miles. River access is down a steep trail around private land. Lower: Follow AZ 88 to AZ 288 which leads north to the river. A short side road before reaching the bridge drops to the river.

FACILITIES: The nearest facilities are located along the highway, in Globe and in other nearby towns.

WILDLIFE: Along with the bald eagles, the river otter (another rare

southwestern inhabitant) has also been reported in this area. Javelina and other desert dwellers are frequently spotted.

CAUTIONS: Do not go past the 288 Bridge RAP. A very dangerous diversion dam is only a short distance downstream. From December 1 to June 30 there is no stopping permitted between river miles 18.6 and 17.3 to avoid disturbing the nesting eagles.

INFORMATION: Tonto National Forest (for river guide and permit applications).

USES:

    Class II   all year   warm   eagles

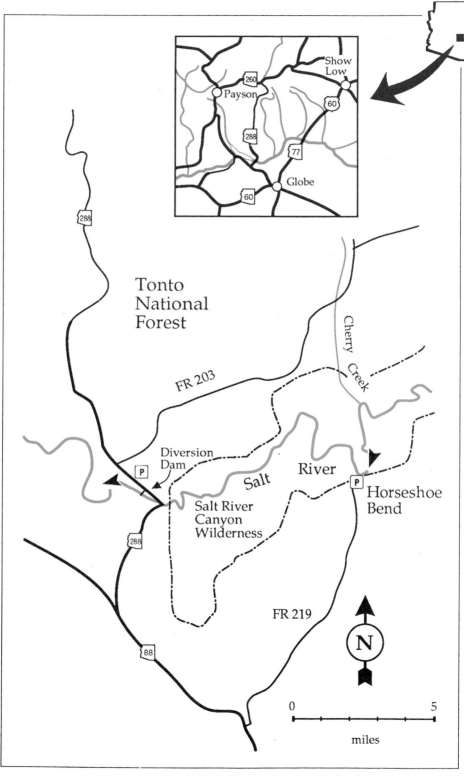

Show Low

Payson

260

60

288

77

Globe

60

288

Tonto
National
Forest

Cherry Creek

FR 203

Diversion
Dam

P

Salt   River

P

Horseshoe
Bend

Salt River
Canyon
Wilderness

288

FR 219

88

N

0   5
miles

East

SALT RIVER —Stewart Mtn. Dam to Granite Reef Dam

LENGTH: **14 miles** SEASON: **All year**
ACCESS: **Paved road** ELEVATION: **1400' - 1300'**
FEATURES: **Long season, easy access, close to Phoenix**
CAUTIONS: **Crowded conditions, diving hazard, camping closure**
MAPS: **USGS -** Stewart Mtn. Granite Reef Dam
        USFS - Tonto National Forest

One of the most heavily used stretches of river in the U.S., this convenient oasis provides one million user-days per year of relief from the blistering hot summers of the 'Valley of the Sun.' In spite of heavy use, the river and its surroundings remain surprisingly beautiful. On a hot summer weekend you can practically walk its length on inner tubes filled with people. But on a weekday or during the off-season (if the litter has been removed), a backcountry experience is almost possible.

Located at the edge of the Superstition Mountains, the scenery is striking, the water is cool and clear. The number of access points make it easy to customize a run to fit a busy schedule (or to escape if the river becomes clogged with tubers). A commercial outfitter rents inner tubes and provides a shuttle bus. So smear on the sunscreen, watch the cliffs for divers, and pack out what you bring in. You can have a good time here.

ACCESS: Follow the Bush Hwy (FR 204) north out of Mesa. The road parallels the river and provides access at several points. Or, drive north out of Scottsdale on the Beeline Hwy 87 and then south past Saguaro Lake to the river via the Bush Hwy.

FACILITIES: Camping is permitted in the Lower Salt River Recreation Area during the off-season (November 1 to March 31). And everything under the sun is available just over the hill in the Phoenix-metro area.

WILDLIFE: The riparian area is host to hundreds of migratory and water loving birds. Dozens of desert species live just beyond its limits. But during the summer the 'Valley of the Sun' party animal may be the most abundant form of wildlife.

CAUTIONS: Glass containers are prohibited here - a quick look at the river bank will tell you why. Wear sturdy shoes while wading. Every year a number of injuries and fatalities occur along this stretch as a result of people jumping or diving from streamside rocks. Avoid life ending or crippling injury - use common sense, step into the water, don't dive into it.

INFORMATION: Tonto National Forest (for river guide).

USES:

Class I/II   warm

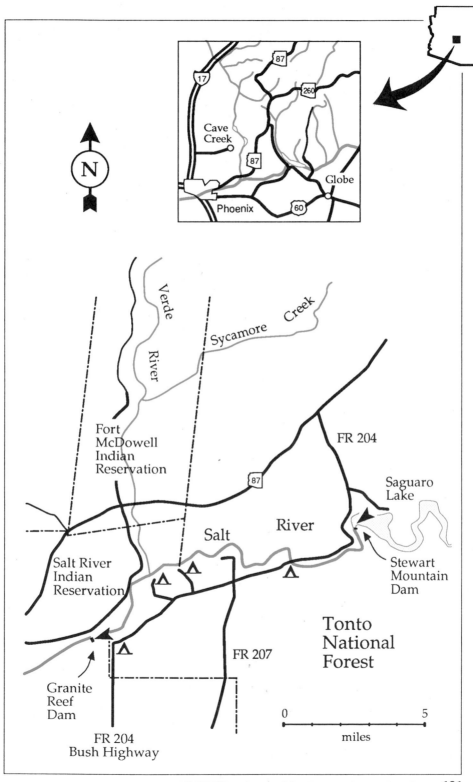

East

SAN FRANCISCO RIVER
— Hot Springs to Clifton

LENGTH: **54 miles**   SEASON: **March — mid-April**
ACCESS: **Paved road**   ELEVATION: **4750' - 3480'**
FEATURES: **Scenic canyon, mild whitewater, hot springs**
CAUTIONS: **Unpredictable season, fences and strainers, ORV closure**
MAPS: **USGS** - Glenwood, Wilson Mtn, Big Lue NE, Harden Cienega, Dix
Creek, Mitchell Peak, Clifton
USFS - Gila National Forest, Apache -Sitgreaves National Forest

T hough it has a short season at best (no season some years), it remains a popular whitewater stream. From the hot springs below Pleasanton, NM to Clifton, AZ is a multi-day run over mild whitewater. The river drops into a narrow, winding canyon cut through country that is extremely remote — one of the premier wilderness river runs in the Southwest. Though clear for the most part, downed trees can stretch from bank to bank, requiring a portage. This run looks like a natural for low water boating.

Birdwatching is also popular. A road leading upstream from Clifton is passable for some distance at low water. Along it you can see threatened Mexican black hawks and wintering bald eagles, with chances for other large birds like ospreys and endangered peregrine falcons. Bighorn sheep have moved down the San Francisco from areas in New Mexico.

ACCESS: Upper: Drive south from Clifton on US 666, north on AZ 78 (which becomes New Mexico 78) to US 180 to the south end of Pleasanton, where a road cuts west to the river. Lower: In Clifton a street parallels the river upstream from the east side of the Clifton Bridge for some distance (changes to dirt).

FACILITIES: A few primitive campsites are at the put-in. Some people camp at a picnic area along the river road in Clifton. Other facilities are available in Clifton.

WILDLIFE: Threatened Mexican black hawks and endangered peregrine falcons can be seen here. Threatened loach minnow are responsible for an ORV closure (state line to the Martinez Ranch). Resident game fish are smallmouth bass and channel catfish.

CAUTIONS: Watch for strainers at high water. The status of the hot springs changes periodically. Enter only if not posted closed. Don't camp near nesting raptors and respect private property boundaries.

INFORMATION: Apache-Sitgreaves National Forest, Clifton Ranger District; Gila National Forest, Glenwood Ranger District

USES:

Class I & II   warm   primitive raptors

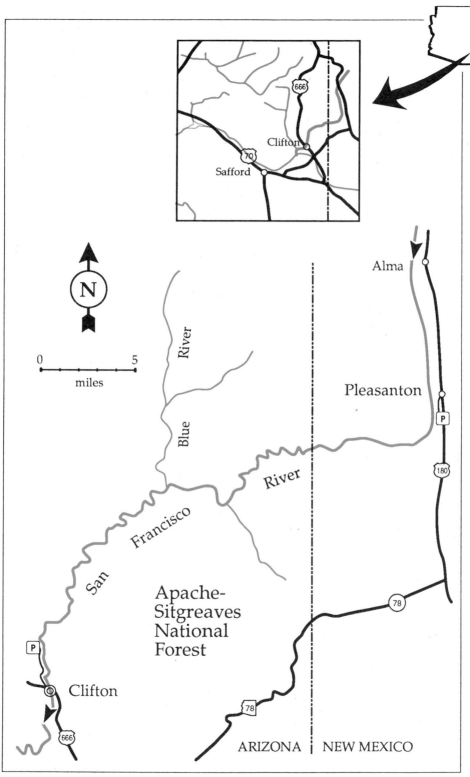

SAN FRANCISCO RIVER

— Clifton to Gila River

LENGTH: **10 miles**
ACCESS: **Dirt road**
FEATURES: **Rare raptors, scenic canyon, easy access**
CAUTIONS: **Low flows, ORV damage, private property**
MAPS: **USGS** - Clifton, Guthrie
      USBLM - Safford District

SEASON: **March — mid-April**
ELEVATION: **3480' - 3300'**

R afting down this stretch is another way to gain access to the fascinating canyon country of the Gila Box. Many river runners prefer starting a Gila Box trip here because it enables them to avoid a couple of parcels of private land and cross-river fences at the head of the Gila run. This river has the same Sonoran-Chihuahuan Desert habitat and wide variety of raptors for which the Gila and Eagle Creek are famous. The whitewater is mild too — more tight turns than big rapids.

Just above the confluence with the Gila, Mexican black hawks nest near the river and petroglyphs decorate the side canyons. In addition to rafting, people come to the San Francisco to hike, birdwatch, and fish for small-mouth bass and catfish. There seems to be low water boating potential.

ACCESS: (From Clifton) <u>Upper:</u> Drive toward Morenci on US 666. Where the road tops a hill, turn south on Mountain View. In half a mile a road turns left (opposite Reservation Street) through a maze of corrals, down to the river. <u>Lower:</u> Drive south 34 miles on US 666, west 3 miles on US 70, north on the San Jose Road 6 miles to the City of Safford Utility Road then east to Bonita Creek Road to the Gila.

FACILITIES: A few primitive campsites are located at the put-in (the "East Plant Site"). There are some primitive campsites at the take-out. Other facilities available in Clifton, Morenci, and Safford.

WILDLIFE: Threatened Mexican black hawks and endangered peregrine falcons can be seen here. Threatened loach minnow swim in the stream. Rocky Mountain bighorn sheep have spread into the area from New Mexico. Sightings of river otters have been reported.

CAUTIONS: Watch for strainers at high water. People who run this river caution against leaving your car overnight at the put-in. Don't camp near nesting raptors and respect private property boundaries.

INFORMATION: U. S. Bureau of Land Management, Safford District; Phelps Dodge Company, Morenci

USES:
    Class I & II   warm   primitive raptors

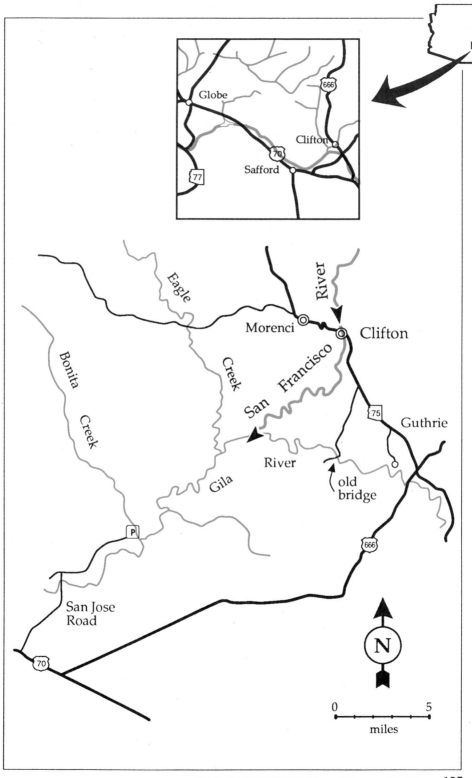

East

WHITE RIVER—North Fork

LENGTH: **15 miles**
ACCESS: **Paved road/dirt road**
FEATURES: **Trout fishing, easily accessible**
CAUTIONS: **Tribal permits required, closed areas**
MAPS: **USGS** - Horseshoe Cienega, McNary, Indian Pine, Alchesay Flat, Whiteriver
 USBIA - Fort Apache (White Mtn Apache) Reservation

his is the White Mountain Apache's showplace trout stream. It is one of the largest streams on the reservation and is heavily stocked and heavily fished. The most popular places to fish are along Upper and Lower Log Roads (off Rts 473 and 260 near Horseshoe Lake) and at Diamond Creek. These locations provide ample camping spaces and easy access. For bigger fish, however, you'll have to hike away from the road.

The setting varies from alpine to desert riparian. As the stream nears Whiteriver it is bordered by small farms and homesites, which limit access. Below Whiteriver, the river is too warm for trout, but smallmouth bass and catfish take their place. In addition to fishing, this area provides abundant wildlife and scenery to watch. You'll find lots of elk, deer, wild turkey, and bear, as well many smaller animals.

ACCESS: Drive north out of Whiteriver on AZ 73, which parallels the river for a considerable distance. Access to tributaries and more remote stretches of the stream are provided by dirt roads heading off to the east. For access to the upper part, take the Upper Log Road or go to Hon Dah then east on AZ 260.

FACILITIES: There are a number of campgrounds and primitive campsites along the Upper Log Road and other access roads. Most don't have water. All require a fee. Camping is permitted only in designated areas.

WILDLIFE: The White Mountain Apaches take good care of their game species. It's easy to see elk and wild turkey here. It's good bear country too. The tribe frequently stocks all major streams with trout.

CAUTIONS: Instead of an Arizona fishing license, a White Mountain Apache permit is required. A permit is required for all recreational activities including picnicking. Camp only in designated areas. Watch for signs marking closed areas.

INFORMATION: White Mountain Apache (Fort Apache) Reservation.

USES:

fee   cold   fee   fee

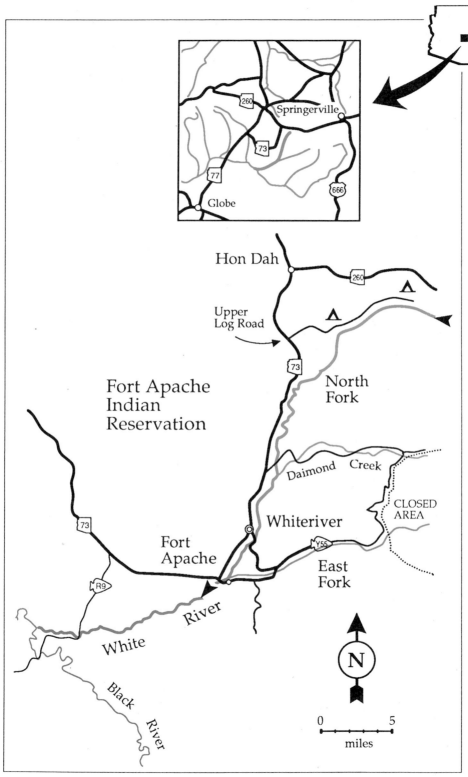

WHITE RIVER — East Fork

LENGTH: **6 miles** SEASON: **Perennial flow**
ACCESS: **Paved road/dirt road** ELEVATION: **6400' - 5000'**
FEATURES: **Trout fishing, easily accessible**
CAUTIONS: **Reservation permits required, closed areas**
MAPS: **USGS** - Odart Mtn, Corn Creek, Bonito Prairie, Elwood Canyon
 USFS - Fort Apache (White Mtn Apache) Reservation

Tumbling down a steep, boulder-strewn chute from the highest reaches of the White Mountains, much of the White River's length is closed to all uses to provide undisturbed spawning for the endangered native Apache trout, *Salmo apache*. It is open to fishing below Reservation Route R30, where it is stocked with rainbow and brown trout. Mostly this is a 'put and take' stream, but some larger fish reportedly lurk in remote pools offering a greater challenge.

Birdwatching is good too, with colorful songbirds like vermilion flycatchers and painted redstarts. A unique aspect of this stream is that many of the trees along its lower alpine stretches are deciduous. That, combined with the boulder-strewn course over which it flows, make the East Fork reminiscent of many streams in the Appalachians of the eastern U.S.

ACCESS: Drive south out of Whiteriver on AZ 73 and turn east toward Fort Apache. This road crosses the river and turns into Route Y55, which parallels the East Fork up to the boundary of the closed area.

FACILITIES: Camping is permitted at a couple of sites along the stream where it is paralleled by the paved portion of Y55. A fee is required even for primitive camping. The best rule is don't camp where signs tell you not to. If in doubt, ask. Other facilities are available in Whiteriver.

WILDLIFE: Colorful birds and colorful fish inhabit the East Fork ecosystem. Here you'll find endangered native Apache trout, a wide variety of migrating songbirds, and abundant game animals.

CAUTIONS: Your Arizona fishing license is useless here. A White Mountain Apache fishing permit is required instead. Permits are also required for all recreational activities including picnicking. Camp only in designated areas. The stream is closed above the R30 - Y55 intersection.

INFORMATION: Fort Apache (White Mountain Apache) Reservation.

USES:

 fee cold fee fee fee

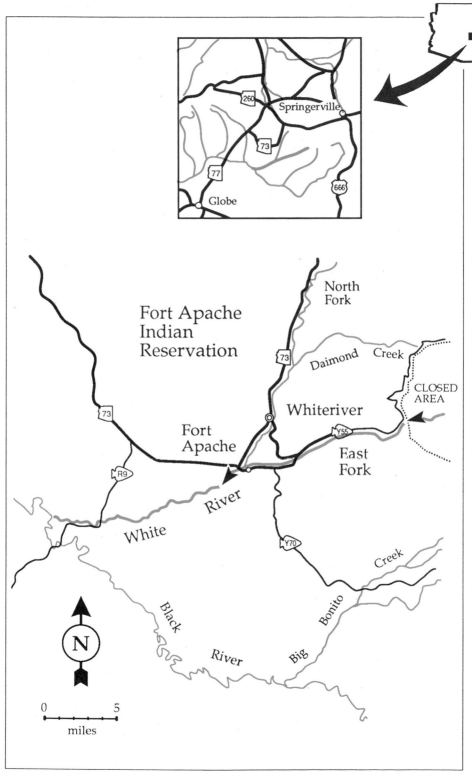

East

Arizona Rivers and Streams Guide

Central Section

Agua Fria River
Cave Creek
East Verde River
Fossil Creek
Granite Creek
Hassayampa River
Oak Creek
Salome Creek
Sycamore Creek
Tonto Creek
Verde River
West Clear Creek
Wet Beaver Creek

AGUA FRIA RIVER

LENGTH: **20 miles**
ACCESS: **Dirt road (HCV)**
FEATURES: **Desert scenery, riparian area, rugged canyon**
CAUTIONS: **Summer heat, private property, fences**
MAPS: **USGS -** New River, Black Canyon City, Squaw Ck Mesa, Joes Hill
　　　USBLM - Phoenix Field Office, (BLM) Bradshaw Mtns-Surface
　　　Mgmt. Maps, Phx. N-Surface Mgmt. Maps.

SEASON: **Intermittent flow**
ELEVATION: **3200' - 1600'**

T he Agua Fria begins as a dry wash in the high desert grasslands east of Prescott. It picks up a moderate flow from a few perennial springs as it drops into a steep basalt canyon. Emerging from the canyon near Black Canyon City, this little river wanders off across the lower Sonoran desert bordered by a strip of cottonwoods, willows, and tamarisks.

This stream attracts people to its sandy beaches and shallow pools for everything from picnicking to watching birds and wading in the pools. Lower reaches may be low water boatable when the spring thaw or a summer monsoon provides adequate flow, but cross-stream fences are a serious hazard.

ACCESS: Leave I-17 at Table Mesa Road (Exit 236) north of Phoenix. Follow the west side frontage road north to a fork in the road (0.5 mile). Both forks lead to the river: the left to State Trust Land which requires a written permit, the right to a couple of primitive campsites and a crossing. Both roads can be impassable if muddy. Other access is via the Rock Springs Interchange. Drive north along the east frontage road.

FACILITIES: There are commercial campgrounds and other facilities at Black Canyon City. Primitive campsites are available along the river.

WILDLIFE: Mule deer, javelina, and bobcat are common. Harris' hawks

like to hunt from the tops of saguaros. Other desert and riparian birds are plentiful. Endangered southern bald eagles nest in the upper reaches of Lake Pleasant.

CAUTIONS: Be aware of land ownership. There are a number of mine sites and other private properties that are both posted and non-posted against entry. A written permit from the State Land Dept. is required at certain access points. Stream quality suffers from heavy grazing and ORV use.

INFORMATION: USBLM, Phoenix Field Office; State Land Dept.

USES:

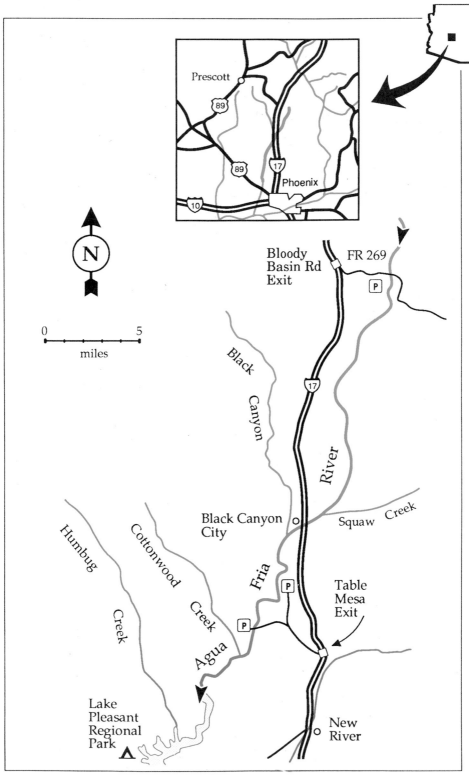

Prescott

89

89

17

Phoenix

10

N

0　　　　　5
miles

Bloody
Basin Rd
Exit

FR 269

P

Black

Canyon

17

River

Black Canyon
City

Squaw　Creek

Humbug

Cottonwood

Fria

Creek

Creek

Agua

P

P

Table
Mesa
Exit

Lake
Pleasant
Regional
Park

New
River

Central

CAVE CREEK

LENGTH: **16 miles**
ACCESS: **Dirt road, hiking trail**
FEATURES: **Scenic desert, cool pools, colorful birds**
CAUTIONS: **Hot summers and sunburn**
MAPS: **USGS -** Humboldt Mtn., New River Mesa, Cave Creek
        USFS - Tonto National Forest

SEASON: **Perennial flow**
ELEVATION: **3320' - 2200'**

T his beautiful little desert stream conveniently close to the Phoenix metropolitan area, is popular enough that nearby Seven Springs campground is usually full. However, since the middle stretches are reachable only via a hiking trail, it is possible to walk away from the crowds. The reward is worth the effort. Cool waters bubble through riffles and plunge over boulders into pools just right for a refreshing dip to escape the desert heat. Songbirds flit through the cottonwoods, cactus wrens chatter from saguaro tops and raptors ride the thermals. You might see anything from the threatened black hawk to a roadrunner. You certainly will see lots of lizards.

The trail is a gentle one that horseback riders use also. You can hike all the way through from Seven Springs to FR 48 or just take a short stroll to the first inviting pool and spend the day.

ACCESS: From Carefree take the Cave Creek Road (FR 24) east past Horseshoe Dam Road (FR 19), beyond where it turns north and changes from pavement to dirt, to Seven Springs Campground. At Seven Springs take FR 24B, the northern-most road through the campground, to a parking lot and trail access.
Lower end: Out of the town of Cave Creek take FR 48 north to its end.

FACILITIES: There are three USFS campgrounds in the area near the confluence of Cave Creek and Seven Springs Wash. They are usually full so arrive early. Other facilities in Cave Creek and Carefree.

WILDLIFE: Cave Creek is an excellent place to birdwatch, especially during the spring migration. It's also a good place to see javelina, coyote, ringtail cats, and mule deer.

CAUTIONS: Arrive early if you expect to camp and be ready to be disappointed, especially in the peak summer months. Take enough water for your hike; the water in the creek is not suitable for drinking. Respect private property boundaries.

INFORMATION: Tonto National Forest, Cave Creek Ranger District; Cave Creek and Carefree Chambers of Commerce

USES:

fee

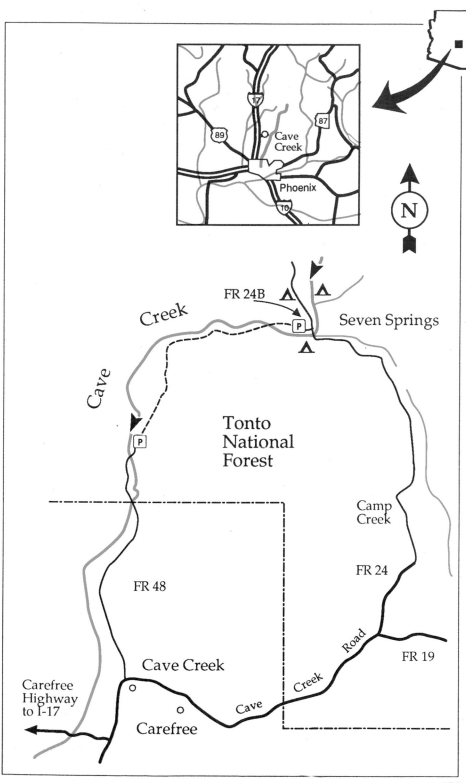

EAST VERDE RIVER

LENGTH: **37.5 miles**   SEASON: **Perennial flow**
ACCESS: **Paved road/dirt road, trail**   ELEVATION: **4535' - 2475'**
FEATURES: **Trout fishing, Wilderness Area**
CAUTIONS: **Extreme isolation, unrunnable waterfalls and slippery rocks**
MAPS: **USGS -** Payson North, Buckhead Mesa, North Peak, Cypress Butte,
       Cane Springs Mountain, Verde Hot Springs
       USFS - Tonto National Forest

T he East Verde is a remote stream that is most heavily used near where it crosses AZ 87. Here it is regularly stocked with trout and attracts a large number of anglers. There is a large campground along a picturesque stretch upstream of the highway and a picnic area downstream. Both offer good opportunities for fishing and water play in the shade of tall cottonwood and willow trees.

The stream becomes increasingly remote as it flows south into the Mazatzal Wilderness. From this point, it is accessible only by way of a primitive trail. Expert boaters have run this stretch, but several unrunnable waterfalls make it a life-threatening undertaking. At its mouth, the East Verde crosses the Verde River Trail #11.

ACCESS: From Payson: Take AZ 87 north 6 miles to the East Verde Bridge, or drive 12 miles on FR 406 to the trailhead at the Mazatzal Wilderness boundary. FR 209 leaving AZ 87 at mile marker 261.5 also provides access to this stretch.

FACILITIES: There is a developed USFS campground north of AZ 87 on Flowing Springs Road and a picnic ground south of the AZ 87 bridge. Other facilities are available in Payson and Pine.

WILDLIFE: Upper reaches of this stream are stocked with trout. Along the lower reaches, javelina and other desert-dwelling animals may be seen.

CAUTIONS: The only access to its confluence with the Verde River is a hiking trail.

INFORMATION: Tonto National Forest, Payson Ranger District

USES:

                            cold   eagles

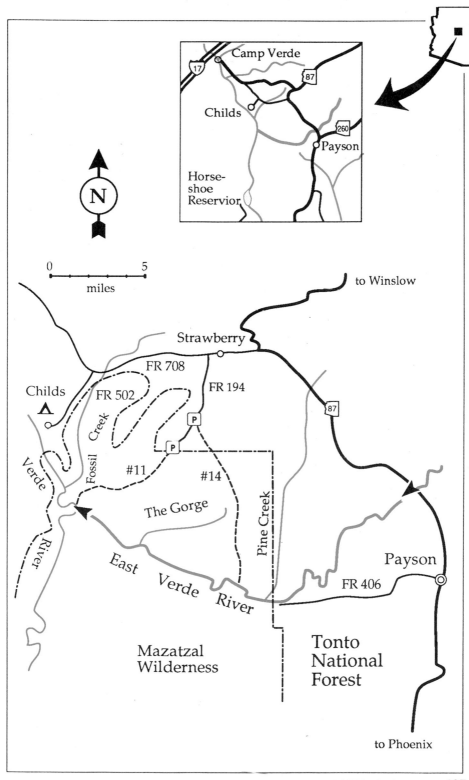

Central

FOSSIL CREEK

LENGTH: 14 miles   **SEASON: Perennial flow**
ACCESS: Dirt Road   **ELEVATION: 4700' - 2560'**
FEATURES: Unique riparian area, historic power plant, Wilderness Area
CAUTIONS: Slippery rocks and sunburn
MAPS: USGS - Strawberry
       USFS - Coconino

T his has been described as one of the most diverse riparian areas in the state. The stream itself seems to appear from nowhere, gushing out of a series of springs at the rate of 20,000 gallons a minute. Over the years, the calcium-saturated waters have laid down a huge deposit of a material called travertine, the same substance that forms stalactites and stalagmites in caves. Most people use Fossil Creek as a place to sunbathe, wade, hike and bird watch. Expert kayakers consider it a serious challenge, rating its difficulty as high as V to VI on a six value scale.

The upper stretches of the creek lie within the Fossil Springs Wilderness Area, while downstream the waters of the creek are captured in a flume that directs them to the turbines of the oldest continuously operating hydroelectric plant in the state.

ACCESS: From Camp Verde: Drive 5 miles on the General Crook Highway, then 15 miles on F. S. 708. Turn left on FR 502 and drive about three miles to FR 154 and the wilderness area trailhead, or turn right and drive 7 miles to Childs.

FACILITIES: There is a USFS primitive campground at Childs. Commercial facilities are available at Camp Verde.

WILDLIFE: The rich riparian area furnishes shelter and nourishment to a wide variety of birds and mammals. Red-tailed hawks abound here, as well as several kinds of warblers and flycatchers.

CAUTIONS: Such a rich and fragile habitat deserves your consideration. Take care to leave it as you found it.

INFORMATION: Coconino National Forest; Beaver Creek Ranger District

USES:

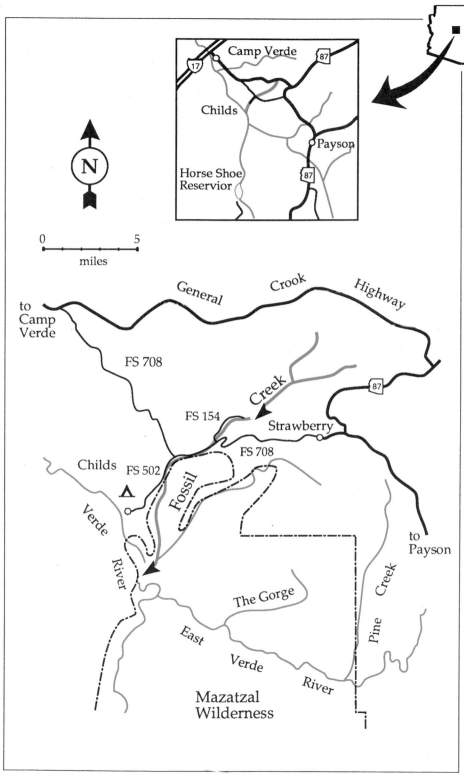

GRANITE CREEK

LENGTH: **6 miles**
ACCESS: **Paved road**
FEATURES: **Urban riparian park, birds, par course, picnic area**
CAUTIONS: **Small size, city setting**
MAPS: **USGS -** Prescott
      USFS - Prescott National Forest

SEASON: **Perennial flow**
ELEVATION: **5619' - 5162'**

This little stream wouldn't attract much attention if it didn't flow right through the middle of Prescott. It does, however, and in the process provides the city with an easily accessible riparian retreat complete with trees full of songbirds and the pleasant babble of running water.

The city has dedicated two parks along Granite Creek. One of these is right in the downtown area. People can take advantage of it even if they have no more time than a few minutes during lunch. The parks provide facilities for exercising, picnicking, nature watching, and horseshoe pitching. A few pools are big enough to entice kids into splashing and wading. Upstream of the city you can hike along the stream in the cool pines of the Prescott National Forest.

ACCESS: Granite Creek Linear Park is located between Gurley and Goodwin Streets in downtown Prescott. A.C. Williams Granite Creek Park is located off of Sixth Street. The White Spar Road (US 89) parallels the stream for about four miles south of town.

FACILITIES: There is a USFS developed campground along the stream on White Spar Road. Other facilities are available in Prescott.

WILDLIFE: Songbirds are of main interest here with crimson, yellow and black western tanagers being among the most colorful.

CAUTIONS: None. The downtown stretch is even lighted at night.

INFORMATION: Prescott National Forest; Prescott Parks and Recreation Department.

USES:

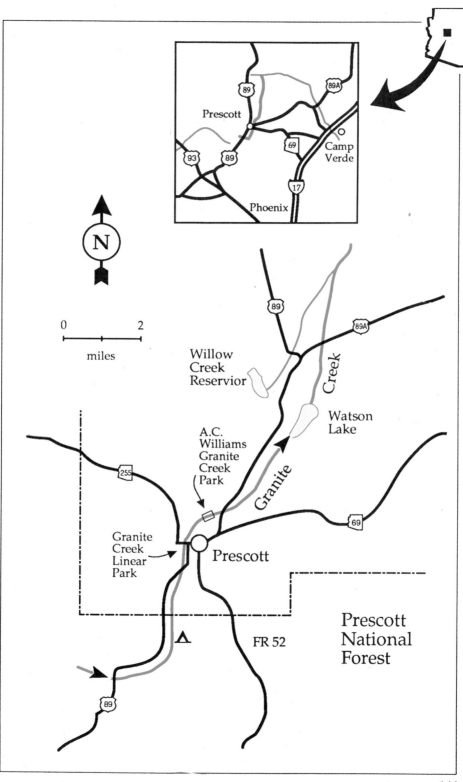

HASSAYAMPA RIVER

LENGTH: **14 miles**   SEASON: **Intermittent flow**
ACCESS: **Paved road/dirt road (HCV)**   ELEVATION: **2250' - 1920'**
FEATURES: **Lush oasis, rich plant and animal diversity, riparian preserve**
CAUTIONS: **Closed areas, fee area, summer heat**
MAPS: **USGS -** Samuel Powell, Cotton Center
       USBLM - Phoenix Field Office, Bradshaw Mtns-Surface Mgmt. Map

T rue to its Apache name, "river running upside down," the waters of the Hassayampa flow beneath the sands of its streambed for much of its length. In a few places, rock layers push that flow above ground, transforming a parched dry wash to an oasis teeming with plant and animal life.

A private conservation group, The Nature Conservancy, owns much of the longest wet stretch near Wickenburg. Though some of the area is closed to enable it to regain its former richness, there is a self-guided nature trail that winds beneath cottonwoods and willows to wildlife watching areas where people can discover just how fertile this habitat can be. North of Wickenburg another wet stretch provides opportunities for picnicking and wildlife watching in the scenic canyon of the Hassayampa Box.

ACCESS: From Phoenix drive northwest on AZ/US 93 (the Wickenburg Highway) to mile marker 116. South of the road is a rest area with access to the river. Two miles upstream is the Hassayampa Preserve. Hassayampa Box: From Wickenburg follow US 93 for 5 mi. Turn east on a dirt road marked Scenic Loop Drive, past a mine site (6.5 mi), turn right to the river.

FACILITIES: There are picnic tables at the ADOT rest area along the river. Other facilities in Wickenburg. Camping is allowed at rest area.

WILDLIFE: Over 240 species of birds have been sighted at the preserve - a good place to see colorful vermilion flycatchers and Abert's Towhee and rare birds like the yellow-billed cuckoo, possibly Arizona's most endangered bird. There are many lizards, one of the more obvious of which is the zebra-tailed lizard, running with its striped tail held high like a scorpion's stinger.

CAUTIONS: Using the Preserve's trails requires a small fee. Much of the area is closed. No picnicking or pets on the main preserve grounds. No motorized vehicles in Hassayampa Box Canyon.

INFORMATION: USBLM, Phoenix Field Office; The Nature Conservancy; Wickenburg Chamber of Commerce

USES:

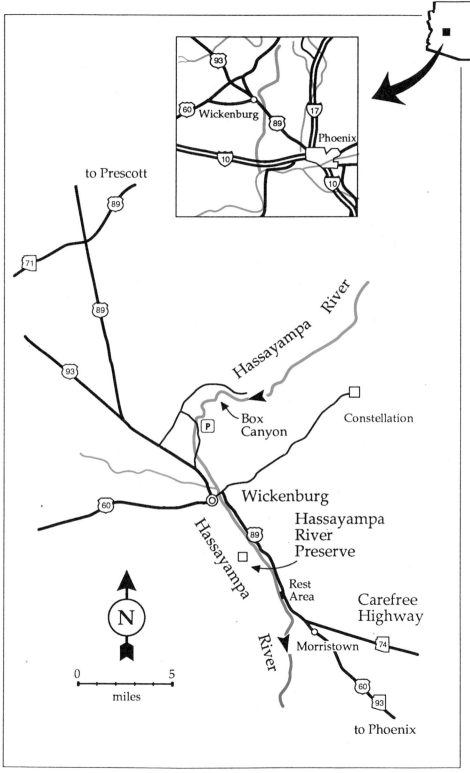

to Prescott

Hassayampa River

Box Canyon

P

Constellation

Wickenburg

Hassayampa River Preserve

Hassayampa River

Rest Area

Carefree Highway

Morristown

to Phoenix

N

0   5
miles

Wickenburg

Phoenix

OAK CREEK — Pumphouse Wash to Sedona

LENGTH: **14 miles**   SEASON: **Perennial flow**
ACCESS: **Paved Road**   ELEVATION: **5689' - 4200'**
FEATURES: **Swimming, fishing, spectacular scenery, easy access, state park**
CAUTIONS: **Slippery rocks, shallow pools**
MAPS: **USGS -** Wilson Mountain, Munds Park, Mountainaire
        USFS - Coconino National Forest

O ak Creek Canyon is known around the world for its striking scenery. Its red, buff and black cliffs soar up to 2500 feet above the canyon floor. Along the creek, numerous pools provide opportunities for swimming and wading. In some places the stream's flow has cut narrow channels in the bedrock to form natural water slides. The most popular of these, Slide Rock, has been set aside as a state park of the same name.

All seasons are worth a visit. In spring, however, migrating birds and blooming wildflowers add interest to any outing and the autumn colors against a backdrop of red rock canyon walls are unmatched. Numerous hiking trails provide access to side canyons and offer dramatic overlooks. One of the most popular of these is the West Fork Trail which provides an easy hike up a spectacular side canyon.

ACCESS: From Flagstaff: Take US 89A south 14 miles. The same route parallels the stream as you drive north out of Sedona.

FACILITIES: Several Natl. Forest Campgrounds are located creekside along US 89A. Restaurants, shopping, commercial campgrounds and other lodging are available along US 89A, in Sedona and Flagstaff.

WILDLIFE: Oak Creek Canyon is an excellent place to watch birds and observe other wildlife species. Animals of special interest are bald eagles, osprey, ring-tailed cats and mule deer. The stream is stocked regularly with trout and offers some large resident fish to challenge experienced anglers.

CAUTIONS: Because the scenery in the canyon is so striking, drivers are often distracted. Drive defensively. The rocks at Slide Rock State Park can be extremely slippery, as are the steeper stretches of the hiking trails. Watch your step. Diving in the shallow pools has resulted in the paralysis of at least one visitor.

INFORMATION: Coconino National Forest, Sedona Ranger District; Arizona State Parks; Sedona Chamber of Commerce

USES:

                                        cold   fee

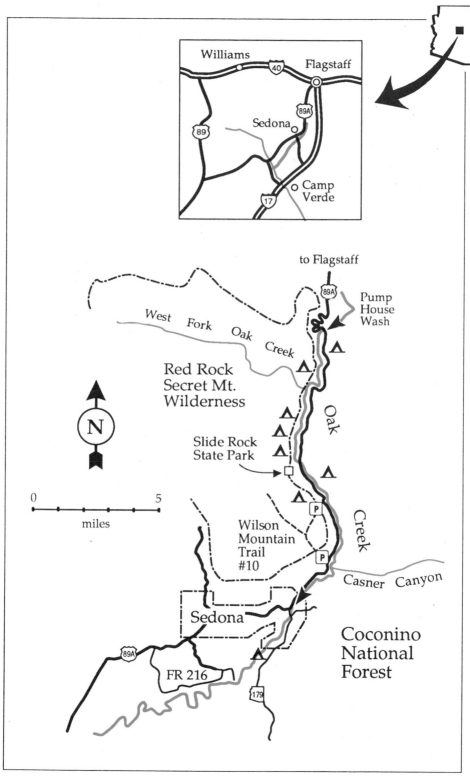

OAK CREEK — Sedona to Verde River

LENGTH: **28 miles**
ACCESS: **Paved road**
SEASON: **Perennial flow**
ELEVATION: **4200′ - 3175′**
FEATURES: **State Park, low water boating, Page Springs Fish Hatchery**
CAUTIONS: **Strainers at high water**
MAPS: **USGS -** Page Springs, Sedona, Cornville
USFS - Coconino National Forest

After Oak Creek emerges from the confines of the canyon at Sedona, it continues through an area of notable scenery all the way to its confluence with the Verde River. Along this stretch is Red Rock Crossing, probably one of the most photographed scenes in the state. Red Rock State Park is set to open a few miles downstream in September 1990. The primary focus of this facility will be on environmental education, but it will offer limited opportunities for picnicking, hiking and fishing.

While previously considered too small to be of interest to river runners, the lower reaches, from Cornville down, have become very popular with low water boaters. A narrow but navigable channel offers year-round access to a beautiful stretch of cottonwood and sycamore lined creek.

ACCESS: Drive west on US 89A from Sedona. About 4 miles from the Rt 179 intersection, turn south on FR 216 (Red Rock Upper Loop Road) for two miles, then either turn left on FR 216 A to Red Rock Crossing, or continue on FR 216 to Red Rock State Park (after late 1990). Additional access is available in Page Springs via FR 134, and in Cornville via FR 119.

FACILITIES: There is a developed campground at Page Springs. Commercial camps, shopping, restaurants, and lodging are available along US 89A and in nearby communities.

WILDLIFE: Lower Oak Creek supports a wide variety of bird species, including threatened Mexican black hawks. River otters reintroduced to the Verde River have spread this far. The stream is home to beaver, threatened roundtail chubs, as well as smallmouth bass and catfish.

CAUTIONS: At high water, trees, log jams, and cross-creek fences can create dangerous strainers. Much of the stream is through private land.

INFORMATION: Coconino National Forest, Sedona Ranger District; Arizona State Parks; Sedona Chamber of Commerce

USES:

warm   fee

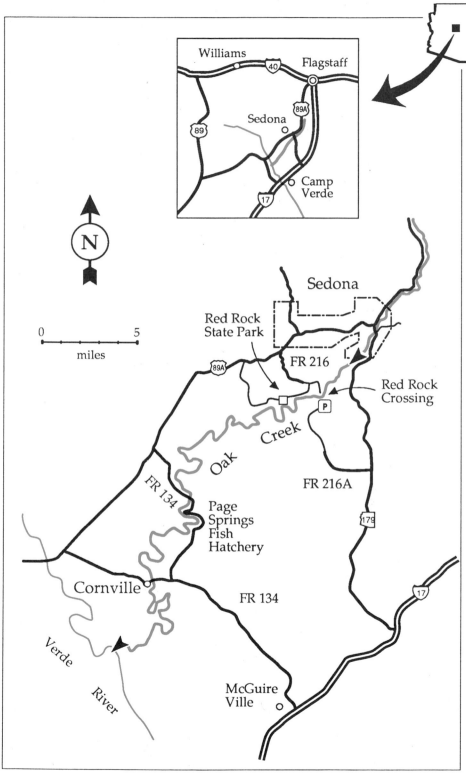

SALOME CREEK

LENGTH: **23 miles**   SEASON: **All year**
ACCESS: **Dirt road (HCV)**   ELEVATION: **4000' - 2136'**
FEATURES: **Scenic canyon, wilderness, trout fishing**
CAUTIONS: **Steep trails, remote area, difficult access**
MAPS: **USGS -** Armer Mountain, Windy Hill
     USFS - Tonto National Forest

L ooking upstream from its lower end, Salome Canyon is an impressive sight. The high peaks of the Sierra Anchas and the conical shaped pinnacles near the mouth of the canyon form an impressive backdrop for the bright green cottonwoods that mark the creek's course as it meanders toward Roosevelt Lake. Though the flow may abe humble here, farther upstream, trout swim in shaded pools between sheer walls. The increasingly constricted streambed serves as the trail leading into the Salome Wilderness. Eventually you are forced to walk in the water, even swim in places (use caution if you opt to do this). You'll find uncrowded trails, secluded swimming holes and isolated campsites.

There is a route into the canyon's upper reaches along a trail that starts at Reynolds Trailhead and drops 1400 feet into a place called Hell's Hole. The trail is steep and rough - not a good place to be on a hot summer day.

ACCESS: From Globe-Miami, take AZ 88 north. Turn on AZ 288 toward Young and after about 9 miles turn left onto FR 60. It's 10 rough miles to Salome Creek. Cross the creek and drive 6 miles to the trailhead of Trail 61, which leads into the canyon. To reach upper Salome, stay on AZ 288 to the Reynolds Creek Trailhead. From here, Trail 284 leads to the Salome Wilderness.

FACILITIES: USFS campgrounds at Rose Creek and Reynold's Creek on the Young Highway (AZ 288). Young has some picturesque old bars and general stores. Other facilities at Globe or Punkin Center.

WILDLIFE: There are trout in Salome Creek wherever there's enough water to support them. Other animals include javelina, bobcat, coatimundi and mountain lion. There are black bears here too, mostly cinnamon colored.

CAUTIONS: Summers here can be very hot, making already steep climbs even steeper. The extreme remoteness can magnify small problems. FR 60 can be impassible when wet. Respect private property.

INFORMATION: Tonto National Forest, Tonto Basin and Pleasant Valley Ranger Districts

USES:
                              cold

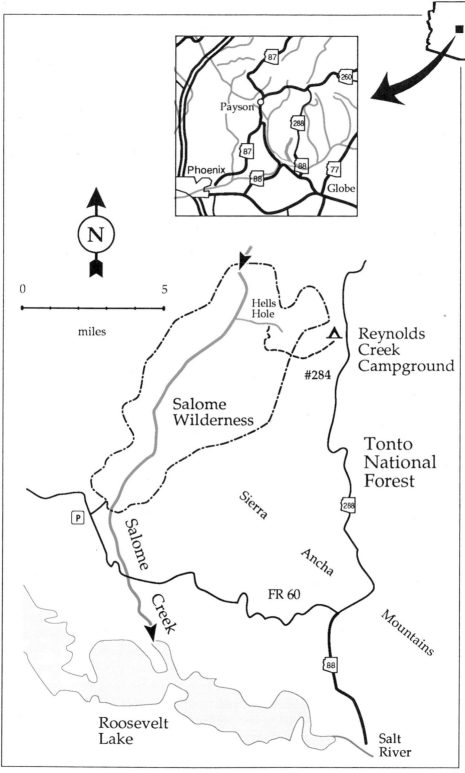

87

260

Payson

288

87

88

77

Phoenix

88

Globe

N

0   5

miles

Hells
Hole

△ Reynolds
Creek
Campground

#284

Salome
Wilderness

Tonto
National
Forest

P

Salome

Sierra

288

Ancha

FR 60

Creek

Mountains

88

Roosevelt
Lake

Salt
River

Central

SYCAMORE CREEK

LENGTH: **16 miles**
ACCESS: **Dirt road**
SEASON: **Perennial flow**
ELEVATION: **3320' - 2200'**
FEATURES: **Desert riparian area, accessible remoteness**
CAUTIONS: **Summer heat, crowded entry, ORV damage**
MAPS: **USGS -** Boulder Mtn, Maverick Mtn, Adams Mesa
USFS - Tonto National Fores

S treams convenient to urban areas tend to be too popular for their own good. In spite of a significant case of overuse in some areas, this pictur- esque bearer of one of the most overused stream names in the state still offers very enjoyable places to picnic, hike, splash in a pool, or sunbathe on a sandy beach. It even offers a few places to relax in pleasant solitude, if you're willing to walk.

On the upper end, you can drive right to a shady streamside campsite under tall sycamores. On the lower end, you can hike upstream past the last evidence of ORV travel and lose yourself among the willows and boulders that dot the stream channel. The crystal clear water flows over a bed of granite gravel in classic Sonoran desert surroundings. The best time is in the spring when the wildflowers are blooming and the songbirds are plentiful.

ACCESS: Turn east off AZ 87 (the Beeline Hwy) at mile marker 218.5 on FR 22, Bushnell Tank Road. This dirt road fords the creek and leads to several primitive campsites. Lower Sycamore: Turn west off AZ 87 at mile marker 204. Drive 3.5 mi. to the stream. An increasingly rough 4WD road leads upstream.

FACILITIES: There are primitive campsites at both access points. (This is a good place to hone your skills at low impact camping.) For all facilities go to Phoenix or Payson.

WILDLIFE: Birds are probably the most common, except for lizards.

Watch the dust for snake tracks - gopher snakes mostly, but no doubt an occasional rattler. Mammals include both mule and whitetailed deer as well as coyote and raccoon.

CAUTIONS: This place is extremely popular with ORV users, especially the lower end. If you are easily offended by noise and fumes don't come on a weekend unless you're willing to walk a ways. Plans are to relocate the highway away from the stream.

INFORMATION: Tonto National Forest, Mesa Ranger District

USES:

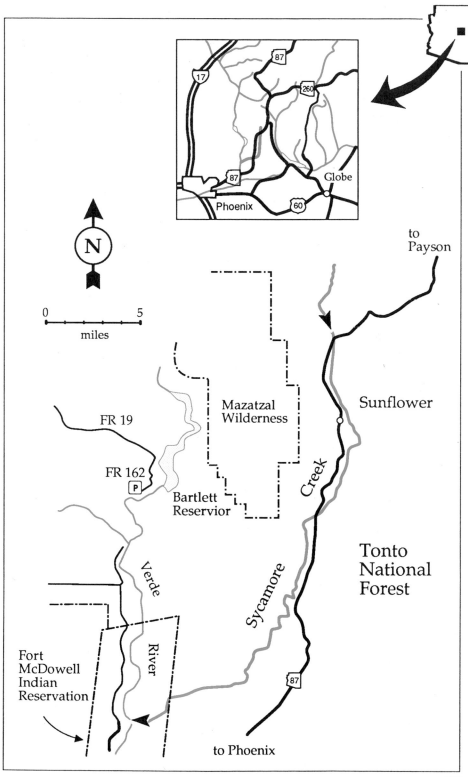

TONTO CREEK — Fish Hatchery to Gisela

LENGTH: **33 miles**
ACCESS: **Paved road/hiking trail**
FEATURES: **Easy access, wilderness canyon, colorful townsite**
CAUTIONS: **Arduous hiking trail, private property**
MAPS: **USGS** - Promontory Butte, Diamond Butte, MacDonald Mtn., Gisela
      USFS - Tonto National Forest

SEASON: **All year**
ELEVATION: **3984' - 2950'**

The upper, easily accessible portion is a popular area for fishing, picnicking, camping and water play. Downstream, the creek drops into a canyon so deep and precipitous that it has been given the name Hell's Gate. Fishing is the main attraction along this stretch of the stream. Since it is a long arduous hike, only the hardy regularly venture here.

Tonto Creek serves as the centerpiece of the Hell's Gate Wilderness until it emerges a couple of miles upstream of the colorful little outpost of Gisela (pronounced Guy-zeela by locals). Gisela consists of a picturesque Old West bar, restaurant, hotel and general store - all under one roof and well worth the visit. Upstream of Gisela, where Tonto Creek exits the Wilderness, the land is privately owned and access is restricted.

ACCESS: From Payson: Follow AZ 260 east 15 miles to FR 289, which parallels upper Tonto Creek. For the Hells Gate Trail, turn off AZ 260 at FR 405A (11 miles east of Payson) and drive 0.3 miles to the trailhead. Gisela may be reached from AZ 87 (Phoenix to Payson Rd) by driving 5 miles east on FR 417. From Gisela follow the Tonto Creek Shores road.

FACILITIES: There is a USFS campground streamside along FR 289 and at the FR 269/AZ 260 intersection. Another is located along Christopher Creek off AZ 260. Some primitive camping is available streamside at Gisela.

WILDLIFE: This is some of Arizona's best black bear and mountain lion habitat. Since this stretch starts in ponderosa pines and ends in saguaros, you're liable to see just about anything along it.

CAUTIONS: The climb into and out of Hell's Gate is strenuous - carry sufficient water. Private land restricts access to some of the lower sections. Trying to hike along the creek can be very difficult and often dangerous within the Wilderness.

INFORMATION: Tonto National Forest, Payson Ranger Dist; Payson Chamber of Commerce; Gisela

USES:

cold   USFS fee area

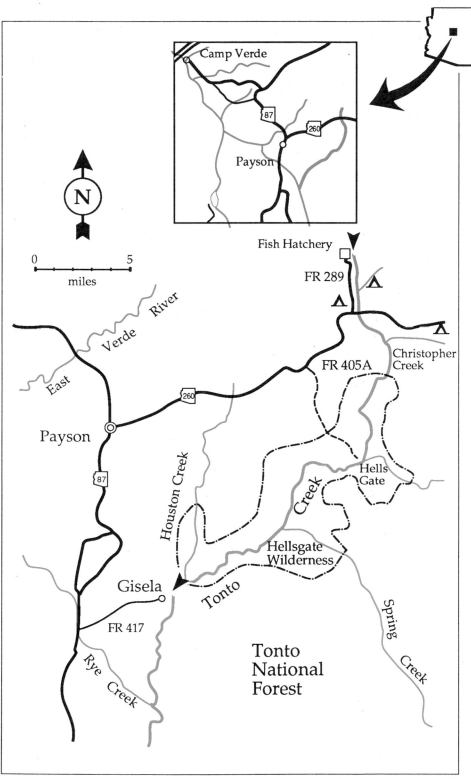

TONTO CREEK — Gisela to Rye Creek

LENGTH: **7 miles**

ACCESS: **Dirt road**

FEATURES: **Rare eagles, scenic canyon**

CAUTIONS: **Cross-stream fences, wildlife closure, private property**

MAPS: **USGS -** Gisela

      USFS - Tonto National Forest

SEASON: **Perennial flow**

ELEVATION: **2920' - 2700'**

B elow Gisela, Tonto Creek drops into another narrow, rocky gorge where the gradient is steep and the waters swift. Some boaters have floated this stretch, but it is runnable only at high water and then it can be quite dangerous. In some places the channel is extremely restricted and it is possible to wedge a boat. In fact, the Forest Service discourages people from running this stretch - it's a boat wrecker.

About three miles below Gisela, entrance is prohibited along the river from Dec. 1 to June 30 to keep from disturbing a nest of endangered southern bald eagles. This effectively closes two access points during that part of the year when the river most likely has enough water in it to run. The lower access point is across private property at the 76 Ranch. Check with the rancher before crossing private land.

ACCESS: From Phoenix drive north on AZ 87 to the Gisela turnoff (FR 417). Drive 5 miles east to Gisela and follow the Tonto Creek Shores Road to the creek. To the lower access, turn south from FR 417 just after it leaves AZ 87. Follow FR 184 about 5 miles to FR 134. Turn east on FR 134 about 1 mile to the creek.

FACILITIES: There is a restaurant, cabins, and general store in Gisela. Some primitive camping is available streamside at Gisela.

WILDLIFE: One of only 22 nesting pairs of bald eagles has taken up residence along this stretch. It is also home to javelina, whitetailed and mule deer, and a good variety of songbirds. Some trout wash down this far from the stocked areas upstream.

CAUTIONS: An area encompassing approximately 1.5 river miles is closed to entry from Dec. 1 to June 30 because of the nesting eagles. The river itself can be quite tricky with strainers and fences. The USFS does not encourage people to boat it.

INFORMATION: Tonto National Forest, Tonto Basin Ranger District; Gisela

USES:

        class III   cold   primitive   eagles

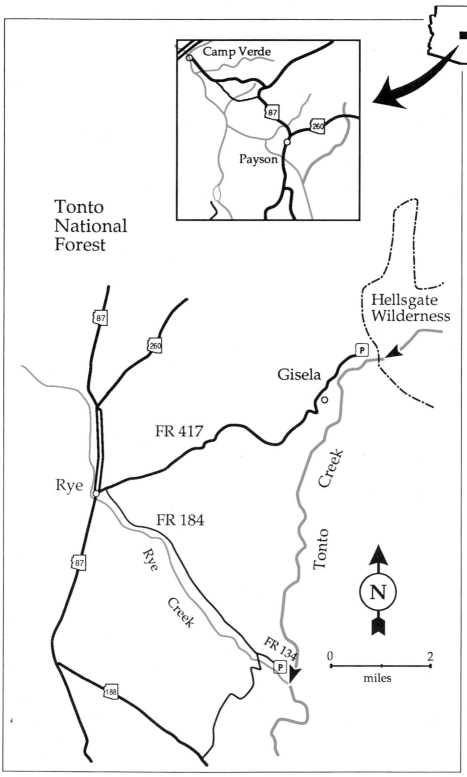

Camp Verde

87

260

Payson

Tonto
National
Forest

87

260

Hellsgate
Wilderness

P

Gisela

FR 417

Tonto Creek

Rye

FR 184

87

Rye Creek

N

FR 134

P

188

0   2
miles

Central

TONTO CREEK — Rye Creek to Roosevelt Lake

LENGTH: **34 miles** SEASON: **Perennial stream**
ACCESS: **Dirt road** ELEVATION: **2700' - 2136'**
FEATURES: **Easy access, colorful songbirds, riparian area**
CAUTIONS: **Fences and strainers, private property, gravel pits**
MAPS: **USGS** - Gisela, Kayler Butte, Tonto Basin
  USFS - Tonto National Forest

After dropping into the Tonto Basin, the stream follows a braided, twisting course across broad gravel bars. In places clear pools hug steep banks shaded by a few cottonwoods. In other places the streambed is nothing more than a sand and gravel quarry field. Cross-stream fences and logjam strainers serve as impediments to boating, but cause no problems to birdwatchers and nature lovers who come here to see great blue herons and migratory songbirds.

Access is provided by a couple of good roads that cross the creek near Punkin Center. Up and downstream of these crossings are some excellent places to birdwatch. Fishing is best in the headwaters of the lake where you can catch largemouth bass and catfish.

ACCESS: From Phoenix drive north on AZ 87 to the Tonto Basin turnoff (AZ 188). Drive south on AZ 188. The road parallels the stream for some distance until it flows into the lake. Access to the stream is provided by FR 71, the Roosevelt Gardens Road and FR 60.

FACILITIES: There are general stores and gas stations in Punkin Center. The nearest developed campground is at Bermuda Flat on Roosevelt Lake. It is a fee area.

WILDLIFE: This is a popular place to birdwatch for songbirds, especially along the lower reaches near Roosevelt Lake. Look for hooded orioles and western tanagers close to the stream. Back in the desert you'll see cactus wrens and Gambel's quail. Hummingbirds are everywhere.

CAUTIONS: Much of the land along this stretch is privately owned. Take note of that as you try to get down to the river. If you do try to float this stream, watch for fences and logjams.

INFORMATION: Tonto National Forest, Tonto Basin Ranger District

USES:

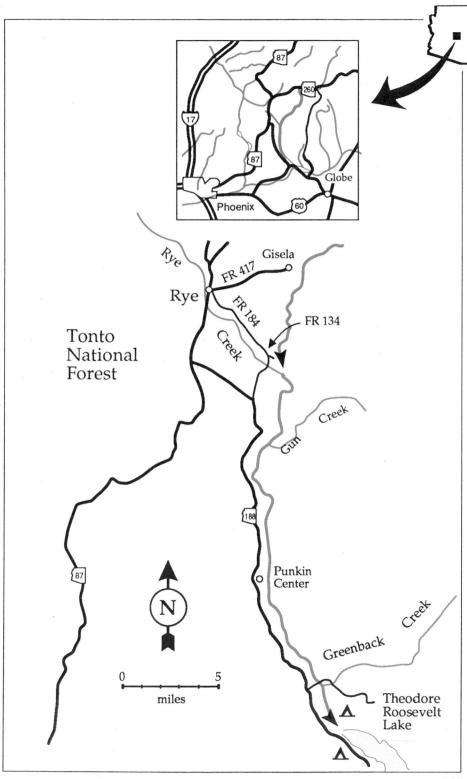

VERDE RIVER — Perkinsville to Clarkdale

LENGTH: **23 miles**
ACCESS: **Dirt road**
SEASON: **Perennial flow**
ELEVATION: **3825' - 3363'**
FEATURES: **Low water boating, hiking, wildlife watching**
CAUTIONS: **Private property, high water strainers**
MAPS: **USGS** - Perkinsville, Sycamore Basin, Clarkdale
        USFS - Prescott National Forest, Coconino National Forest

This stretch of the Verde River has begun to attract interest as a low water boating run. The best times to run it are in the spring, when the snows of the nearby mountains are melting, or in late summer after a monsoon rain. Actual dates of runnable flows remain unpredictable. A railroad parallels the river and is used as a hiking trail.

Just downstream of Perkinsville, cottonwoods provide a nesting side for a great blue heron rookery. The river here is on private property but it is possible to get good views of the birds and their nests from the railroad bed. The river continues past cliffs and caves of redwall limestone, the same stratum that forms the tallest cliffs within the Grand Canyon. From the confluence of Sycamore Creek to the diversion dam near Clarkdale the river is always above 55 cfs and low water boatable.

ACCESS: From Williams: South 23 miles on FR 173, then County Road 70 for 8 miles to the Perkinsville bridge. From Jerome: County Road 72 for 14 miles, then FR 354 to the bridge. From Clarkdale: Tuzigoot Natl. Monument Road to the river.

FACILITIES: Camping, shopping, restaurants and lodging are available in Clarkdale, Cottonwood, and Williams.

WILDLIFE: There is a large great blue heron rookery just down river of Perkinsville that provides special interest. Endangered southern bald eagles also nest along this stretch. The stream supports a warm water fishery including threatened roundtail chubs and spikedaces. Antelope, mule deer, otter and black bear may be sighted along its banks.

CAUTIONS: A dam and gravel pit obstruct the river just upstream of Clarkdale. It must be portaged. Some people use an alternate take-out on private property at Tapco to avoid the dam. Access at Packard Ranch at Sycamore confluence is limited by private property.

INFORMATION: Prescott National Forest, Chino Valley and Verde Ranger Districts; Coconino Nat. Forest, Sedona Ranger District

USES:

Class II   warm

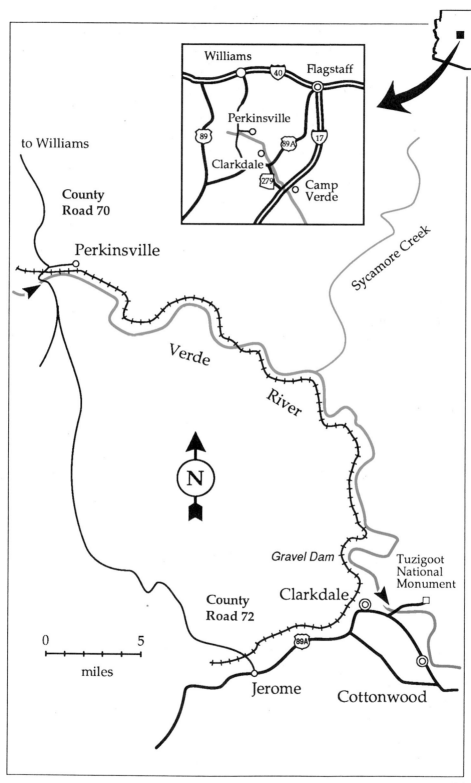

Central

VERDE RIVER — Clarkdale to Camp Verde

LENGTH: **24 miles**   SEASON: **October — April**
ACCESS: **Paved road**   ELEVATION: **3363' - 3147'**
FEATURES: **State Park, National Monument, easy access**
CAUTIONS: **Diversion dams, gravel pits, private property**
MAPS: **USGS -** Cottonwood, Cornville, Middle Verde, Camp Verde
         USFS - Prescott, Coconino

This stretch of the Verde River flows through an area of small farms and suburban ranches. As a result, the stream's waters are heavily used for irrigation. Nevertheless, the river remains a valued recreational resource which attracts considerable interest and is experiencing an ongoing enrichment program. A number of river access points, hiking and biking trails, and picnic sites are being added to those already available. During the winter the Arizona Game & Fish Department stocks the stream with trout.

In spite of heavy use, there are riparian areas along this stretch that remain healthy and attractive. A number of out-of-the-way swimming holes and fishing spots provide popular recreation sites. Arizona State Parks manages the Verde River Greenway to protect the fragile cottonwood-willow riparian forest — one of the rarest ecosystems in North America.

ACCESS: Take the Tuzigoot National Monument Road off AZ 279 just south of Clarkdale, or drive north from AZ 279 on US 89A to the Bridgeport Bridge. For a take-out, leave I-17 at the Middle Verde Exit, turn west and follow a gravel frontage road along the west side of I-17 a short distance to the river.

FACILITIES: Camping is available at Dead Horse Ranch SP. Commercial camps, shopping, restaurants, and lodging is available along Highway 279 and in nearby communities. Canoe rentals are available in Cottonwood and Camp Verde.

WILDLIFE: This riparian area harbors a large number of bird species. Waterfowl are occasional visitors as are bald eagles and ospreys. Raccoons, otters and other small mammals frequent the area.

CAUTIONS: Diversion dams create life threatening hazards at high water. They must be portaged at any level. Several gravel pits obstruct the river. Take out upstream of I-17 to avoid the biggest of these.

INFORMATION: Salt River Project (for flows - 273-5929); Prescott Natl. Forest, Verde Ranger Dist; Coconino Natl. Forest, Sedona Ranger District; Dead Horse Ranch State Park

USES:

Class I   all   fee   fee

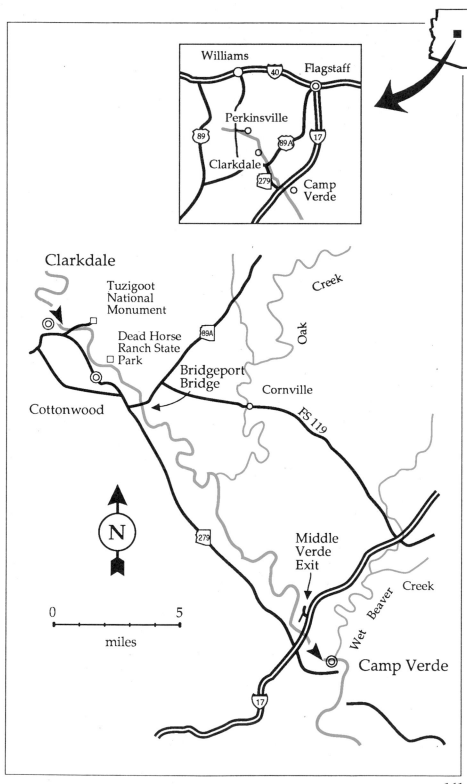

Williams

Flagstaff

Perkinsville

Clarkdale

Camp Verde

Clarkdale

Tuzigoot National Monument

Dead Horse Ranch State Park

Bridgeport Bridge

Cornville

Cottonwood

FS 119

Oak

Creek

N

0   5

miles

Middle Verde Exit

Wet Beaver Creek

Camp Verde

VERDE RIVER — Camp Verde to Beasley Flats

LENGTH: **9 miles**
ACCESS: **Paved road/dirt road**
FEATURES: **Easy access, long season**
CAUTIONS: **Private property**
MAPS: **USGS** - Camp Verde, Horner Mountain
USFS - Prescott, Coconino

SEASON: **All year**
ELEVATION: **3147′ - 3020′**

The major appeal of this segment of the Verde River is its mellow nature and easy accessibility. For the most part, this is a flat water stretch that includes a few easy to run riffles. Low water boaters consider it to be navigable in all but the driest of times — as close to a year-round run as is possible for a small desert river.

Along the way the surroundings change from suburban to rural to remote. Herons nest in the large streamside cottonwoods and osprey fish the river's deep, long pools. People fish here too. This stretch has produced some exceptional shovelhead catfish and largemouth bass. Many people have started great friendships with the Verde along these nine short miles.

ACCESS: <u>Put-in</u>: The General Crook Highway crosses the river at the south end of Camp Verde. <u>Beasley Flats</u>: From Camp Verde take Salt Mine Road 8 miles, then left to the turn-around at the river.

FACILITIES: Commercial camps, shopping, restaurants, lodging and a canoe livery are available in Camp Verde. A USFS campground is located nearby off the General Crook Highway at West Clear Creek.

WILDLIFE: A number of species of raptors, songbirds and waterfowl can be seen along this stretch, including osprey and endangered southern bald eagles. There are also small mammals like raccoons, beaver and, perhaps, even river otters, a species recently reintroduced into this area. Both warm and cool water fish inhabit the river.

CAUTIONS: Much of the land bordering this stretch of the Verde is privately owned. Residents' privacy should be respected.

INFORMATION: Salt River Project (for flows - 273-5929); Prescott National Forest, Verde Ranger District; Coconino National Forest, Beaver Creek Ranger District

USES:

Class I   all

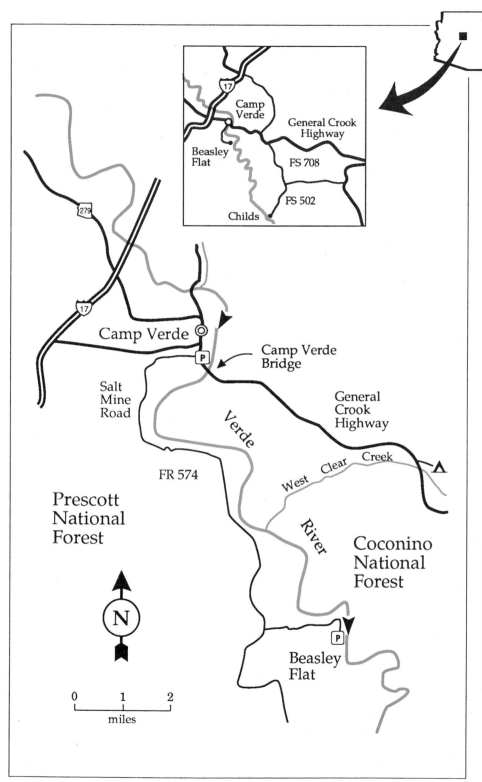

VERDE RIVER — Beasley Flats to Childs

LENGTH: **18 miles**   SEASON: **October - April**
ACCESS: **Dirt road**   ELEVATION: **3020' - 2695'**
FEATURES: **White water, bald eagles, river otters, hot springs**
CAUTIONS: **Waterfall, rapids, wildlife and ORV closures**
MAPS: **USGS -** Camp Verde, Horner Mtn., Hackberry, Verde Hot Springs
         USFS - Coconino, Prescott, Tonto, Recreation Opportunity Guide

T his is the most challenging white water run on the Verde River. Variable flows make its season extremely unpredictable. On good snow years the high water season can last from late February to mid-April. Other years may provide no boating at all. The use of plastic canoes and small inflatable boats can extend the river running season on this segment to include all but the driest of times.

This stretch of the Verde is Arizona's only Scenic River Area which is a component of the Federal Wild and Scenic Rivers system. It is excellent for fishing, wildlife watching and hiking. Numerous access points are available by foot, horseback and 4WD. Of the latter, the most popular is at Gap Creek, 9 miles downstream of Beasley Flats.

ACCESS: (From Camp Verde)
Beasley Flats: Salt Mine Road 8 miles then left to the turn-around at the river. Childs: Hwy 260 for 5 miles, then FR 708 for 15 miles and FR 502 for 7 miles.

FACILITIES: Primitive campsites and toilets located at Childs. Commercial facilities are available in Camp Verde. There is an undeveloped hot springs near Childs.

WILDLIFE: Bald eagles are frequently seen; also look for rare river otters (reintroduced here in the early 1980s).

CAUTIONS: Scout *Verde Falls* & Turkey Gobbler Rapid. Portaging is usually recommended at Verde Falls. Wet suits are advisable. To avoid disturbing nesting eagles *no stopping is permitted for 1.5 miles below the falls* (Dec. 1 to June 15). Gap Creek is closed to off-road-vehicles.

INFORMATION: Salt River Project (for flows, 236-5929); Prescott National Forest, Verde Ranger District; Coconino National Forest, Beaver Creek Ranger District; Tonto National Forest.

USES:

Class III   warm   eagles

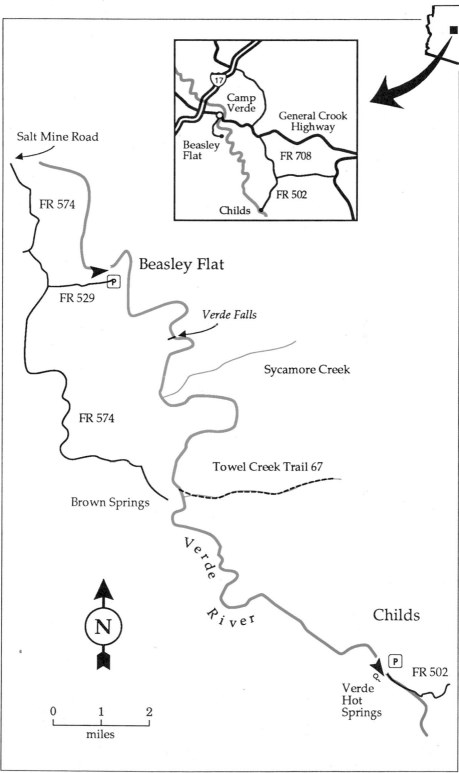

Salt Mine Road

FR 574

Beasley Flat

FR 529

Verde Falls

Sycamore Creek

FR 574

Towel Creek Trail 67

Brown Springs

Verde River

Childs

N

Verde Hot Springs

FR 502

17

Camp Verde

General Crook Highway

FR 708

Beasley Flat

FR 502

Childs

0   1   2
miles

Central

VERDE RIVER — Childs to Horseshoe Reservoir

LENGTH: 35 miles   SEASON: **October - April**
ACCESS: **Dirt road (HCV)**   ELEVATION: **2695' - 1995'**
FEATURES: **Wild River Area, Wilderness Area**
CAUTIONS: **Extreme isolation, high water strainers**
MAPS: **USGS -** Verde Hot Springs, Wet Bottom Mesa, Chalk Mtn.
     USFS - Tonto National Forest visitors map, Recreation Opportunity
     Guide

T his stretch of the Verde stands out as the only federally designated Wild River Area in Arizona. Here the river is extremely remote for the entire stretch with no access but hiking and horseback trails. Bald eagles soar above it and mountain lions prowl the mountains that border it. This is truly a wilderness river.

The boating season on this stretch of the Verde consists of two parts. First, the big water season for rafts and kayaks lasts as long as the snow melt. In some years that may amount to only a few days. The low water boating season continues much longer. For those willing to drag a canoe over a gravel bar the experience of running this stretch of river can be enjoyed almost year-round.

ACCESS: Childs: Take Hwy 260 for 5 miles from Camp Verde then FR 708 for 15 miles to FR 502 and 7 miles to Childs. Sheep Bridge (just above Horseshoe Reservoir): Take Bloody Basin exit from I-17. Follow FR 269 for 32 miles.

FACILITIES: USFS primitive campgrounds are located at Childs & Sheep Bridge. Other facilities are available in nearby towns. There are undeveloped hot springs at Childs and Sheep Bridge.

WILDLIFE: Riparian birds include the bald eagle. The stream holds both large and smallmouth bass as well as channel and flathead catfish. Javelina and mule deer are common.

CAUTIONS: Small problems can be magnified by the amount of time and trouble it takes to get help. Watch for strainers.

INFORMATION: Salt River Project (for flows - 236-5929); Coconino Natl. Fores, Beaver Creek Ranger District; Tonto National Forest, Cave Creek Ranger District.

USES:

Class II   warm

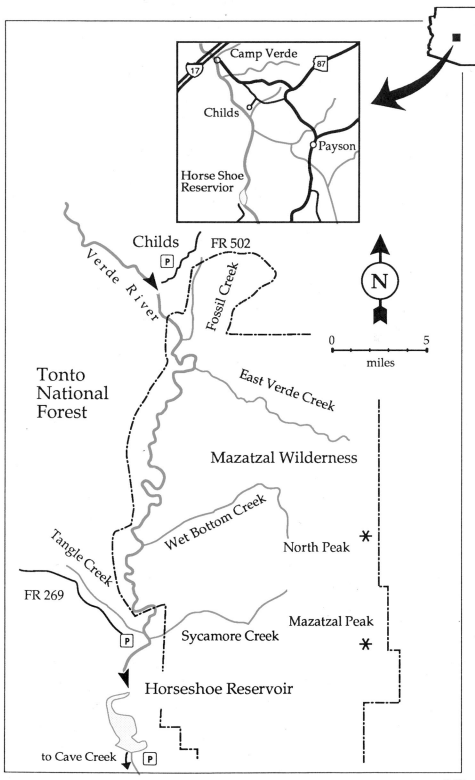

VERDE RIVER — Horseshoe Dam to Bartlett Res

LENGTH: **20 miles** SEASON: **All year**
ACCESS: **Dirt road** ELEVATION: **1897' - 1750'**
FEATURES: **Remote setting, Sonoran desert habitat**
CAUTIONS: **Rugged access, long flata water stretch, wildlife closure**
MAPS: **USGS -** Horseshoe Dam, Lion Mtn., Maverick Mtn.
 USFS - Tonto National Forest

This stretch is significant because of its remote Sonoran desert surroundings. The run is a fairly easy one with a shuttle that is not as long or rough as the stretch just upstream. The flow of the river depends entirely on the release from Horseshoe Dam. Call the Salt River Project for current information. The rapids are easy but there are a few strainers to watch for at high water. Four miles below Horseshoe Dam, boaters are prohibited from stopping near a nesting site of endangered bald eagles.

To avoid the three hour paddle across Bartlett Lake some people use the alternate access at Devil's Hole (4WD only). Another solution is to bring a motor. The river and the lake provide good fishing for catfish and bass.

ACCESS: (From Cave Creek) <u>Put-in</u>: Take FR 24 for 7 miles, to FR 19. Follow FR 19 for 6 miles to FR 205 and turn left. Follow FR 205 for 6 miles to Mesquite Flat Campground. <u>Takeout</u>: FR 24 to FR 19, follow FR 19 for 13 miles, to FR 459 and 3.5 miles to Bartlett Flats.

FACILITIES: There are USFS primitive campgrounds at Horseshoe Reservoir and at Bartlett Reservoir. Other facilities are available at the nearby communities of Cave Creek and Carefree.

WILDLIFE: A number of bird species inhabit the riparian areas along the river. Beavers swim in its

waters. The stream supports a warm water fishery including largemouth and smallmouth bass as well as channel and shovelhead catfish.

CAUTIONS: At high water the river can be clogged by dangerous strainers. From Dec. 1 to June 15 *stopping is prohibited near a bald eagle nesting site four miles downstream of Horseshoe Dam.* The paddle across Bartlett Reservoir can take as much as three hours.

INFORMATION: Salt River Project (for flows - 236-5929); Tonto National Forest, Cave Creek Ranger District

USES:
 Class II warm

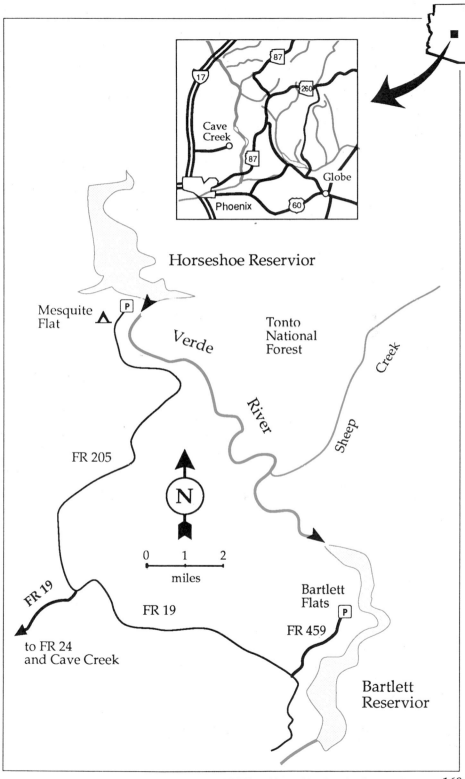

VERDE RIVER — Bartlett Dam to Salt River

LENGTH: **24 miles**
SEASON: **All year**
ACCESS: **Dirt road/paved road**
ELEVATION: **1600' - 1325'**
FEATURES: **Easy access, regular flows, bald eagles**
CAUTIONS: **Crowded camps, wildlife closure, Indian Lands**
MAPS: **USGS -** Bartlett Dam, Fort McDowell, Granite Reef Dam
      USFS - Tonto National Forest

T his stretch is popular with boaters, largely because the river's flow is regulated by Bartlett Dam. In addition, the upper portion of this run offers a pleasantly remote desert setting with enough small riffles and eddies to make the paddling interesting. It's a good place for bird and wildlife watching and the smallmouth bass fishing isn't bad. The shuttles are fairly long but usually possible in passenger cars.

The several points of access along this stretch make the length of any trip adjustable. As it nears the Salt River, the Verde passes through the Fort McDowell and Salt River Indian reservations. Be sure to check with the tribes before crossing their land.

ACCESS: (From Cave Creek) <u>Put-in</u>: Follow FR 24 for 7 miles, then FR 19 for 13 miles to FR 162 which leads to the Riverside Campground. <u>Take-out</u>: Follow Pima Road to Pinnacle Peak Road to Rio Verde Road to FR 20 to Needle Rock. Other access is south of the bridge within the Salt River Indian Reservation.

FACILITIES: There are USFS primitive campgrounds available at both Bartlett Dam and at Needle Rock. Facilities are available nearby in Scottsdale and Phoenix.

WILDLIFE: Endangered southern bald eagle nesting site near put-in. Good fishing for catfish, small and largemouth bass. Great blue herons, javelina and coyotes are common.

CAUTIONS: *No stopping is permitted for 3 miles downstream of the put-in* (Dec. 1 to June 30). Check with Fort McDowell Indian Reservation before crossing their land. Entrance is prohibited on the Salt River Indian Reservation.

INFORMATION: Salt River Project (for flows - 236-5929); Tonto Natl. Forest; Fort McDowell Indian Reservation; Salt River Indian Reservation

USES:

Class I   warm   fee   eagles

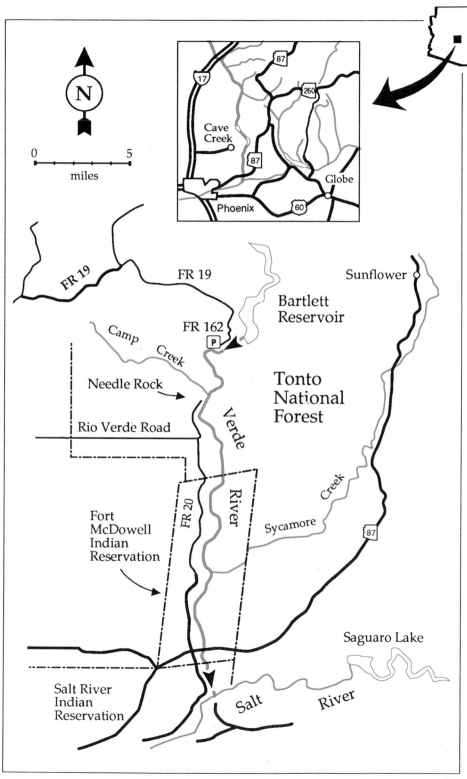

WEST CLEAR CREEK

LENGTH: 40 miles **SEASON:** Perennial flow
ACCESS: Trail, dirt road, paved road **ELEVATION:** 5900' - 3000'
FEATURES: Wilderness area, trout fishing, swimming holes
CAUTIONS: Extreme isolation, cold water, steep trails
MAPS: USGS - Walker Mtn, Buckhorn Mtn, Calloway Butte
　　　　USFS - Coconino

West Clear Creek Canyon presents an exceptional opportunity to experience a desert riparian environment in a relatively undisturbed condition. Hiking the full length of the canyon can be quite an adventure. The only trail for much of the trip is the stream bed and several long swims are required as the creek snakes back and forth between sheer sandstone walls.

If you're not interested in a four or five day backpack, both ends of West Clear Creek Canyon offer some excellent day hiking. The upper reaches of the stream in the vicinity of the Maxwell Trail are known for good trout fishing; the lower portions offer broad swimming holes with sandy beaches. Low water boaters run the stretch from the developed campground to the Verde confluence at intermediate flows.

ACCESS: Maxwell Trail: From mile marker 298 on the Flagstaff-Clints Well Hwy (FH 3), follow FR 81 for 2.9 miles, then FR 81E for 5.8 miles. Bullpen Trailhead and Camp: Follow Gen. Crook Hwy from Camp Verde, then FR 618 for 2 miles, then FR 215 for 3.5 miles. Clear Creek Campground is located 5 miles from Camp Verde on Crook Hwy.

FACILITIES: There is a USFS primitive campground at Bullpen and a developed camp at the General Crook Hwy. Commercial camping and other facilities (including a canoe rental) are available at Camp Verde.

WILDLIFE: Endangered peregrine falcons are sometimes sighted in the canyon. So are bald eagles and a number of other bird species. Black bear, mountain lion, mule deer and elk inhabit the forested slopes.

CAUTIONS: Cold water and long swims (responsible for at least one fatality) can make hiking here very demanding. Bring flotation for your pack for any extended hike in the upper reaches. Flash floods are a hazard.

INFORMATION: Coconino Natl. Forest, Beaver Creek Ranger District; Camp Verde Chamber of Commerce

USES:

cold

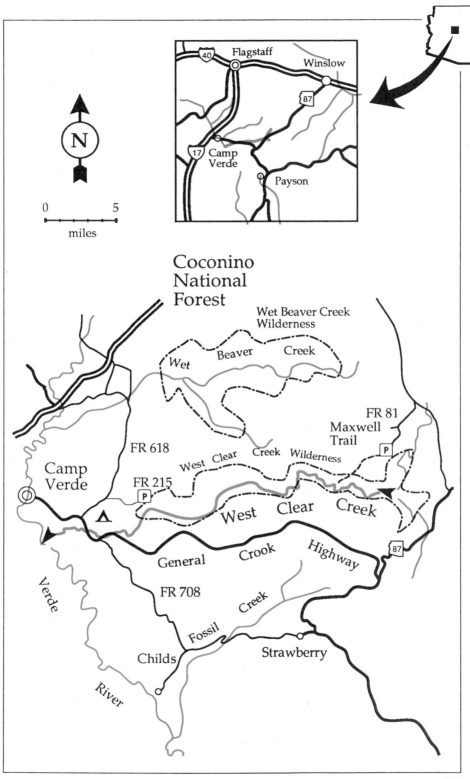

WET BEAVER CREEK

LENGTH: **22 miles**
ACCESS: **Dirt road**
FEATURES: **Wilderness area, hiking trail, swimming holes**
CAUTIONS: **Isolation, one-way access, strenuous hike**
MAPS: **USGS** - Casner Butte, Apache Maid Mountain
      USFS - Coconino

SEASON: **Perennial Flow**
ELEVATION: **3900' - 3075'**

L ike its more famous cousin, Oak Creek, Wet Beaver Creek flows through a scenic red rock canyon. However, along this stream you won't find a road nor the crowds that such convenient access brings. Visitors to Wet Beaver Creek have to work to enjoy the scenery, but the reward is well worth the effort.

The Bell Trail leading upstream starts as an old jeep track and becomes a foot path near the wilderness boundary. Where the trail crosses the stream to climb the canyon's south wall there is an excellent swimming hole and sites for primitive camping. There are also a number of popular water play areas near the USFS campground on FR 618. Below Montezuma's Castle this stream is suitable for low water boating on an opportunistic basis.

ACCESS: <u>Trailhead</u>: Leave I-17 at the Sedona/Oak Creek Exit. Travel east about three miles on FR 618 to the Beaver Creek Ranger Station, then left to the parking lot. Other access is available via the I-17 Middle Verde Exit (to Montezuma's Castle) and from the Middle Verde Road at Verde River Bridge.

FACILITIES: There is a USFS campground along the creek at FR 618. Other facilities are nearby in Camp Verde and McGuireville.

WILDLIFE: A variety of bird species populate the riparian area including the threatened Mexican

black hawk. Lizards, roadrunners and javelina live among the desert scrub. Whitetailed deer, mule deer, and elk inhabit the uplands. The stream is stocked with trout.

CAUTIONS: Mountain bikes are not permitted beyond the wilderness boundary. Hiking more than a mile or so upstream of the Bell Trail requires swimming. High water strainers are a hazard to boaters on lower reaches.

INFORMATION: Coconino National Forest, Beaver Creek Ranger District; Camp Verde Chamber of Commerce

USES:

cold

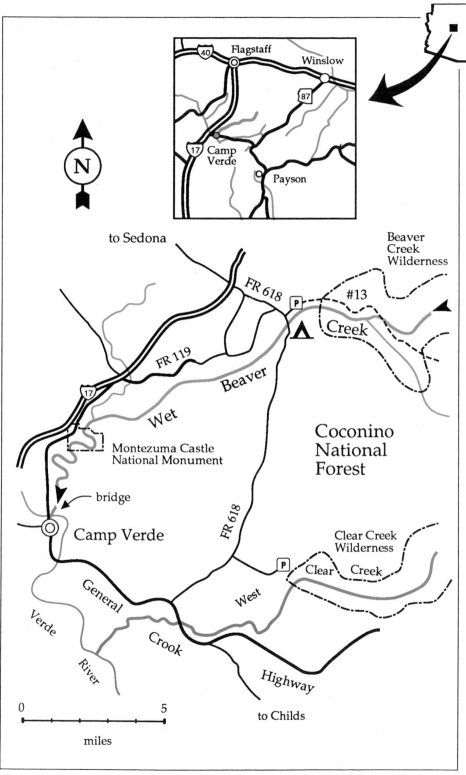